Those Preaching Women

Volume 3

Those Preaching Women

AFRICAN
AMERICAN
PREACHERS
TACKLE
TOUGH
QUESTIONS

Ella Pearson Mitchell, editor

Judson Press ® Valley Forge

Those Preaching Women, Volume 3

Unless otherwise indicated, Bible quotations in this volume are from *The Holy Bible,* King James Version. Scripture quotations marked NRSV are from the NEW REVISED STANDARD VERSION of the Bible, copyright © 1989 by the Division of Christian Education of the National Council of the Churches of Christ in the United States of America, and are used by permission. Scripture quotations marked TLB are from *The Living Bible,* copyright © 1971. Used by permission of Tyndale House Publishers, Inc., Wheaton, IL 60189. All rights reserved.

"Case Dismissed" © by Jacquelyn Donald-Mims.

Library of Congress Cataloging-in-Publication Data
(Revised for vol. 3)
Those preachin' women.
    Vol. 3 is entitled: Those preaching women.
    Contents: [1] Sermons by Black women preachers — v. 2 More sermons by Black women preachers — v. 3 Black Women Preachers Tackle Tough Questions.
    1. Sermons, American. 2. Women clergy. I. Mitchell, Ella Pearson.
BV4241.T475 1985   25285-4731
ISBN 0-8170-1073-4 (pbk. : v.1)
ISBN 0-8170-1131-5 (v. 2)

Printed in the U.S.A.
05 04 03 01 01 00 99
10 9 8 7 6 5 4 3 2

Contents

Preface

A Prefatory Tribute

W hen my wife first asked me to serve as editorial consultant, second-guessing her editing of this volume, I was hesitant. The title *Those Preaching Women, Vol. 3* could easily suggest to some that this is just another collection of women's sermons. Now, of course, until women get "equal time," the fact that these are sermons by women would be cause enough to go to press. This volume, however, grows out of much more than an eager effort to give women exposure. Volume 3 is focused on controversial issues, or perhaps better stated, prophetic utterance. The women who wrote sermons for this book are not just sharing their "best sermons"; they are tackling the hardest questions facing the Christian church. This means, of course, that they have agreed to submit the kind of messages that are most difficult to write.

The difficulty of the task these women have undertaken is laudable enough, but it deserves still further appreciation in view of the fact that very few of these authors are in full-time or single-vocation ministries. Most of them earn livings in secular occupations. And their involvement in these fields suggests impressively high levels of skill in fields far distant from theology— fields like engineering, computer technology, and electronic communications, as well as social work, business, government, and education (ranging from elementary to graduate school).

In other words, we have here the usual situation: African American women are routinely required to be superhuman. We have seen them support and raise families. We have seen them hold demanding jobs and then be awesome wives and mothers.

And now we see seventeen of these women demonstrating their gifts as prophetic preachers who deal with life's most perplexing issues. Their efforts, to say nothing of their successes, are impressive.

Finally, I as a homiletician take my hat off once more to this group of women preachers, for a number of these sermons have succeeded in making the Bible come alive. The minister may find this book profitable for more than its ingenuity in addressing thorny topics. The male minister in particular may actually learn a way to escape the trap of abstraction and offer experiential encounters with the word.

A word is also due my wife. I finally accepted service as official consultant on this project with an undercurrent of fear that I just might be getting exploited a little. Then came the greatest load of work ever to pass through our shared office. Alongside Ella's seventeen sermons were qualifying papers for fifteen D.Min. students, which had to be picked over carefully. I happen to hate that task, and Ella happens not to mind. Not only that; she can find a gnat's eyebrow at a distance of ten feet. So we traded off.

I read the sermons and she read the papers, both of us virtually around the clock. Our Jack-Sprat-and-wife arrangement expedited the record volume of work. And two spouses in their late seventies turned out to be none the worse for wear. In fact, there was an undercurrent of comradery and pleasure as we engaged in hours and hours of what might have been drudgery, side by side in our private sweat shop. A three-day vacation in Bermuda helped greatly, too. All in all, it was a blessed experience I almost missed.

I only hope that the readers of this book will enjoy and profit from these pages as much as I have.

—Henry H. Mitchell

Contributors

Regina C. Anderson is principal of Greenforest Christian Academic Center, Atlanta, and is retired from the administrative staff of the Oakland, California, public schools. She holds a B.A. from Dillard University in New Orleans; an M.Ed. from California State University, San Francisco; an M.Div. from American Baptist Seminary of the West, Berkeley; and a D.Min. from United Theological Seminary, Dayton.

Karen E. Black-Griffin teaches on the faculty of Beulah Heights Bible College and is vice president of PanCentric Systems, Inc., a consulting firm, both in Atlanta. She holds a B.A. from Kent State University, Ohio; an M.S.W. from Howard University; an M.Div. and a D.Min. from The Interdenominational Theological Center, Atlanta. She has served on the staff of several churches.

Linda Boston is pastor of a Lutheran Church in the San Jose area. She holds a B.A. from California State University, San Francisco; an M.Div. from Pacific Lutheran Seminary, Berkeley; and a D.Min. from United Theological Seminary, Dayton. She serves as a regular guest panelist on "The International Sunday School Lesson" broadcast in Chicago.

Elizabeth Mitchell Clement serves as team pastor at the First Congregational Church, Atlanta. She holds a B.A. from Talladega College and an M.Div. from Candler School of Theology, Emory

University. She has served as staff member for President Jimmy Carter, interpreter for the Atlanta Olympic Committee, and project director for the South African Olympic Pavilion.

Beletia Marvray Diamond is on the faculty in religion at Spelman College. She earned a B.A. from Edwards Waters College, Jacksonville, and an M.Div. from The Interdenominational Theological Center, Atlanta. She received her D.Min. from United Theological Seminary, Dayton.

Emilygail Richardson Dill is assistant minister at St. Johns A.M.E. Church in Bermuda, where her husband is pastor. She also teaches senior English and civics at Whitney Institute, a secondary school there. She is a graduate of Spelman College and The Interdenominational Theological Center in Atlanta. She is chairperson of Women in Ministry and the Board of Christian Education of the Bermuda Conference of the A.M.E. denomination.

Jacquelyn Donald-Mims is founder and pastor of the Imani A.M.E. Church, Austin, Texas, and works in strategic alliances for IBM in Austin. She holds a B.S. from Tuskegee University; an M.B.A. from Georgia State University; an M.T.S. from the University of Dallas; an M.Div. from Perkins School of Theology, Southern Methodist University; and a D.Min. from United Theological Seminary, Dayton.

Lillian Frier-Webb is pastor of Mt. Olive A.M.E. Church in Port Washington, New York, and international president of A.M.E. Women in Ministry. She has received degrees from Hunter College, New York City; Adelphi University, Garden City, New York; and Blanton-Peale Graduate Institute, New York City. She is a practicing psychotherapist in West Hempstead, New York, and former columnist for *Essence* magazine.

Teresa L. Fry is assistant professor of homiletics at Candler School of Theology, Emory University, and assistant pastor of St. Paul A.M.E. Church in Lithonia, Georgia. She holds B.S. and M.S.

degrees in speech pathology from Central Missouri State University and M.Div. and Ph.D. degrees from Iliff School of Theology, University of Denver. Her dissertation dealt with the intergenerational transmission of spiritual values through mothers and grandmothers.

Janette Hightower is assistant pastor of St. John United Methodist Church, Berlin, New Jersey, and teaches in the Philadelphia public school system. She is a graduate of Temple University and Eastern Baptist Theological Seminary in Philadelphia, and holds a D.Min. from United Theological Seminary in Dayton. She is a certified marriage and family therapist.

Marjorie B. Lewis serves as associate minister of Macedonia Baptist Church in Denver and is a professor in the Graduate School of Public Affairs, University of Colorado, Denver. She holds a B.A. from the University of Maryland, College Park; an M.B.A. from S.E. University, Washington, D.C.; an M.A. from American Baptist Seminary of the West, Berkeley; a D.Min. from United Theological Seminary, Dayton; and a Ph.D. from Carnegie Mellon University, Pittsburgh.

Kathi E. Martin is pastor of First Immanuel A.M.E. Church, Decatur, Georgia, and associate manager for a major telecommunications corporation. She holds a B.S. in engineering technology from New Jersey Institute of Technology, Newark, and an M.Div. from The Interdenominational Theological Center, Atlanta. Part of her professional responsibilities involve equal opportunity issues, and she is active in AIDS ministries.

Ella Pearson Mitchell is visiting professor and teaches homiletics at The Interdenominational Theological Center in Atlanta. She holds a B.A. from Talladega College, Alabama; an M.A. in religious education from Columbia University Teachers College and Union Theological Seminary, New York City; and a D.Min. from School of Theology, Claremont, California. She is editor of two previous volumes of *Those Preaching Women*.

Normal L. Phillips is an ordained elder at New beginnings Full Gospel Baptist Church, a policy officer for the Social Security Administration, and executive director of Reaching Out to Senior Adults, all in the Atlanta area. She holds a B.S. from Alabama State University, Montgomery; a graduate certificate in gerontology from Georgia State University; and an M.Div. from The Interdenominational Theological Center, both in Atlanta. She has a D.Min. in pastoral care from McCormick Theological Seminary, Chicago.

Classy Preston is pastor of the Pleasant Grove United Church of Christ and sales manager with Carolina Power and Light, both in Raleigh. She earned a B.A. in business administration at Ottawa University, Kansas, and an M.Div. from New York Theological Seminary, New York City. She has participated in Black Executive Exchange and is on the business council of St. Augustine College, Raleigh.

Tina T. Saxon is founding pastor of Disciples Baptist Church and works as a counselor in Project New Life, a drug-addiction treatment program, both in Jamaica Plain, Massachusetts. She earned a B.S. from District of Columbia Teachers College; an M.Ed. from Howard University, and an M.Div. and D.Min. from Andover Newton Theological School. She taught in the Washington, D.C., public school system for many years.

Maxine Merrick Walker is chaplain at Greenville Memorial Medical Center, Greenville, South Carolina, and associate minister at Cedar Grove Baptist Church, Simpsonville, S.C. She holds a B.A. from the University of Central Florida, Orlando, and an M.Div. from The Interdenominational Theological Center, Atlanta. She is working toward national certification as a clinical pastoral educator.

> *Question: Regardless of the validity of all the marvelous modern gains made in the liberation of women, do we dare deemphasize or downgrade the importance of motherhood?*

Faithful Mothers: Stewards of the Spirit

Regina C. Anderson

Pericope: 1 Samuel 1:1-28

For this child I prayed; and the LORD has granted me the petition that I made to him. Therefore I have lent him to the LORD ... (1 Samuel 1:27-28 NRSV).

More often than not, an African American celebrity—whether an athletic hero, Emmy award winner, or recipient of some signal honor—will begin the acceptance remarks by thanking "God and my mama." In the most devastating, demoralizing crime cases, you can almost always see someplace in the distant surroundings, or hear the comments of, a mother, the common denominator of both struggles and joy, who though embarrassed and disheartened is still the mother.

The Bible is inexhaustibly entwined with mothers—faithful mothers—from Sarah, the mother of Isaac and *of* all nations, to Mary, the mother of Jesus, honored *by* all nations. Among them all is an unusual mother whom I'd like you to meet. You may have met her a long time ago but knew her only from afar, having never really gotten to know her and embrace her as a kindred spirit, having never looked at her life beneath the surface.

1

You know the story about the Levite Elkanah and his wife, Hannah. It's a love story, because Elkanah loved Hannah dearly. But she was barren and bore him no sons. In those days, a woman's value was determined by her ability to have a child, especially a son. Elkanah, a godly man to be sure, had waited and waited for a son, as had Abraham, but finally he took himself a second wife, Peninnah. This polygamous arrangement was permissible, but Elkanah did not love Peninnah as he loved Hannah. He simply took Peninnah to be his second wife, because every Hebrew adult desired to have a son. And Peninnah bore him many sons.

Even though Elkanah constantly reminded Hannah of his love for her, that she was his first and greatest love, she grieved and grieved, praying constantly, without ceasing. Her barrenness made her feel inadequate—less than. She wanted to be the head woman of her house, but she couldn't. Her self-esteem was in a bottomless pit! In her spirit, she questioned God, saying over and over, "Why me, Lord?" But she heard no answer. There was silence. Still, she kept the faith. It was as if she knew beyond a doubt that God—only God—understood her agony and pain, her heartbreak!

It was the custom during those days for families to go on a pilgrimage to the annual sacrifice at the tabernacle at Shiloh. Women, though they were at the temple, remained on the outside, while men went in to pray. (You see, women were not the vehicle of prayer.) Elkanah would make a thank offering, and the family would eat together at the feast. Peninnah, because she had so many children, would always get a much larger portion than Hannah.

Hannah would look on with envy. Tears streaming down her face, she would sulk and sulk, with disgust and envy, quiet in desperation. Peninnah, resentful of being second place in Elkanah's life, would taunt and laugh at Hannah, making her cry. Elkanah worried about Hannah; somehow, the reassurance of his love was not enough. Hannah, in spite of the ridicule, just continued to pray night and day, quietly, not speaking a word out loud. She consumed herself in prayer. Her quiet spirit cried out to God, but her countenance revealed her pain.

One day, Hannah entered the temple near the priest and dared to violate those sacred traditions and established practices: She offered her own prayers to God. The priest thought, surely she was drunk. He stared at her. Her mouth was moving but not a word was being uttered aloud. She was drunk (yes, drunk!) with courage! She was in somber and mournful communication with God—internal, unuttered, unspoken. The fervency of her prayer was remarkable. Her patience and long suffering prevailed. Yes! She was drunk with faith that God would intervene for her—a woman.

The scripture says, "The prayer of the upright is his delight" (Proverbs 15:8 NRSV). Hannah had made a vow to God in her prayerful communication that if God would give her the desire of her heart—a son—she would give God the child and the praise. She prayed:

> Dear God, if after these barren years you would overcome all my bodily handicaps and give me a child, I'd be so careful to give the child back to you and to give you the praise! I'll consider your will for him with deepest respect, far above all others—even more, dear God, if you say so! He'll grow up under Eli the priest in the sanctuary, in the temple! He'll be yours, not mine, dear God! Thank you, Lord! I claim and hold sacred the blessings of motherhood, but I realize its limits! I vow to give the child back to you! Thank you, Lord! Amen.

Hannah, in her faithfulness, her belief in God's unfailing love, took her problem to the Lord in prayer. Because of her patience, trust, devotion, and faith in God, Hannah was finally blessed to have a son, whom she named Samuel (which means, "asked of God"). Now, Hannah in her prayers had committed herself, had made a promise, had made a sacred vow to place the child in the temple where he would grow up in favor with God! She couldn't—wouldn't—turn from God! God blessed her, cast away her barrenness, and Hannah praised the Lord for this blessing.

For years, Hannah did not go to the ritual feast at the temple. She stayed home until Samuel was about six or seven years old. Time passed, but she did not forget her promise to God. When Samuel had been fully weaned, she took him to the temple, together with a bull, some flour, and a skin of wine, saying, "I prayed for this child! God answered my prayers, and now I give him back to God!"

Samuel stayed in the temple with Eli the priest. He grew up in the temple in favor with God. Samuel's mother loved him dearly, but she loved God even more! She gave up the dearest and nearest thing to her, her first born, but God continued to bless her to have more children—three sons and two daughters!

Hannah had faith and hope. She was, like my parents, confident in God's greatness and might. And she saw herself as a steward of God's blessings. She acknowledged by her actions that no child belongs to us. We are just vehicles, or channels, that God uses to express life. As much as we love our children, we do not have ownership of them, but we are merely caretakers and stewards! *All* children belong to God! Kahlil Gibran, in *The Prophet,* says:

> *Your children are not your children.*
> *They are the sons and daughters of life's longing for itself.*
> *They come through you but not from you,*
> *And though they are with you yet they belong not to you.*

Incidentally, Hannah alone made the prayerful decision to offer the son that she bore to God. The Scripture does not speak of her husband, who needed a son to perpetuate his name, interfering or disagreeing with her decision to give the child back to God. When Hannah told Elkanah what she was going to do, he said, "Do what seems best to you" (1 Samuel 1:23 NRSV).

Samuel grew up in the temple. His mother visited him once a year, bringing him coats and clothes to wear. His mother's prevailing spirit of prayer and faith remained apparent and charted his life, even in her absence. Samuel grew up in God's favor and became the last and greatest of the judges of Israel. What a blessed and proud mother Hannah must have been! She never regretted her faithfulness. She never regretted keeping her promise to God. Even in death, she must have enjoyed a blessed peace, because she had given her first born back to God.

Hannah was not unique in her decision to give a child to God. I remember a sermon on mentoring I preached entitled "Hangin' 'Round With Old Folk." I cited Elizabeth and Mary, Ruth and Naomi, Paul and Timothy—all relationships in which younger people were guided by faithful servants, stewards of life, and who ultimately gave their guided lives to God. God has blessed me with a mothering-mentoring spirit that has brought joy to my life, as over the years as I have nurtured young men and women in secular education and ministries of Christian service. My prayers acknowledging God's ownership, like Hannah's, have been the foundation on which I stand. My soul cries out in praise as those whom I have nurtured make contributions across the country as leaders—teachers, school administrators, Christian educators, ministers.

There is a belief among the Ashanti, of Ghana in West Africa, that every person has a "kra," an individual identity, unlike anybody else's. (The Yoruba in Nigeria have a similar belief about an "ori.") This kra or unique character is given to every child just before he or she leaves heaven to be born on earth. It is set by God, who according to the Ashantis is very strict about punishing people who tamper with a child's kra. So the Ashanti people let a child be and do what the child is inwardly driven to do. The kra of each child is highly respected. Every child is thought of as a "child of heaven" who never did actually belong to its earthly parents. In spite of the pains of childbirth, mothers are just stewards, vessels used to carry and bring forth life.

One day, I was sitting with some teachers in training, looking through a one-way glass at a university's demonstration nursery school for two-year-olds. We were noting the behavior of children. As we watched the children play in the sand, we heard the comments of the parent-observers inside. They went something like this: "Look at him! He's strong-willed, determined. She's such a lady. She has empathy for his friend. He wants to have his way! Self-willed! Self-oriented!" These comments and a multitude of others like them were about each child's kra, indicative of the child's character before he or she began to relate to the environment of "Don't!" "Share!" "Wait!" Kra is a part of each one of us adults also; it lies deep within. The Ashanti people respect the kra in everyone. If only we ambitious American parents would move out of the way and let God's gift of character unfold in our children's lives!

Hannah, though not an Ashanti, knew that the kra within Samuel was created and controlled by God. She could release him: She had nothing to fear! She had been a vessel—a special vessel—used by God! And so she sang, "My heart exults in the LORD; my strength is exalted in my God."

You might not be a natural mother, having given birth to a child, but if in some small way you have been influential in the life of one of God's children, you have abundant life. Male or female, natural or surrogate parent, you do not need to have a controlling interest in a child to be richly fulfilled. Indeed, selfish clinging to the young frustrates their own purposes. The joy is in releasing them and watching them fly.

I feel that God has blessed me by placing me in an environment where I can provide educational experiences and Christian influence for countless boys and girls. Over the years, the lives of more children than I dare to calculate have been entrusted to me. Sometimes in the lateness of the evening or the early part of the morning, my mind goes back to faces I have not seen for years. My thoughts dance through the personalities that I once knew. I wonder "Where?" and "What?" And often I think, "I should have…" But in spite of what I have done or not done, given or not given, the most important thing to remember is the kra in each of those precious ones. And the most exciting news concerning them will always be how their kra unfolded.

The crowning satisfaction of my life has come in the last year here in Atlanta, where I minister as principal of a Christian academy. For here, without a disguise (Praise God!), I can do what Hannah did. I can openly pray, give the children up, and offer them back to God, that is, lay them at the temple, which is next door to the school. Our whole program can be devoted to acknowledging the kra in every boy and girl, with an assurance that each one was given by God! We only plant the seeds! We are only vessels! Like the prayer and care and stewardship of Mother Hannah, our names might recede into the background. But the children, as did Samuel, will go on to new heights of leadership and service. And even to the Lord, they are a joy forever.

Question: The perennial frustration in our hood is how to get us to work together long enough to marshal what resources we have and solve our pressing problems. What does it take to get us to trust each other and forget glory long enough to get something done?

So We Rebuilt the Wall

Karen E. Black-Griffin

Pericope: Nehemiah 4:1-9

So we rebuilt the wall, and all the wall was joined together to half its height; for the people had a mind to work (Nehemiah 4:6 NRSV).

I grew up in a community that had a strong sense of unity, a community that had a commitment to its members and a very deep concern for the welfare of all. The community that I grew up in was deeply concerned about its future. However, that deep concern for righteousness and fairness seems to be rapidly drifting away, if it has not left altogether already. So then, how do we stir up this deep concern and genuine desire to bring wholeness back to our community and all the similar communities, or hoods, as we say? There was a man by the name of Nehemiah who was confronted with the same dilemma.

Nehemiah, son of Hacaliah, was an honorable man who held a most influential position within the Persian court. He did not join the first wave of returnees to Judah, as did some, after the Babylonian destruction of Jerusalem. Instead, he held on to the most prestigious position of cupbearer to King Artaxerxes. As the cupbearer, Nehemiah was so trusted that he had to sample the king's wine first, to ensure that it was safe from poison. Also, a cupbearer would generally engage in lighthearted and entertaining chats with the king. While in the company of the king, through casual conversation, Nehemiah could make suggestions from time to time that would benefit his comrades.

Nehemiah had a strong concern for his people and a sincere sense of religious zeal and duty. He was always anxious to hear about the progress of the Jews back home. Every now and then he would receive visitors from Jerusalem. These visits made him especially happy, because he held a quiet nationalistic bond with his brothers and sisters in Judah. One day his brother Hanani and a few other brethren showed up at the Persian king's palace. Nehemiah served them some food and gave them a place to rest. He and his brother talked about family matters briefly, and then, all of a sudden, the tone of the discussion changed.

Nehemiah began to ask questions about what was happening with the family's ancestors' graves. Hanani and the others dropped their heads. They admitted that the graves were grown over with weeds, and that Jerusalem in general was in worse shape now than it was when the Babylonians first destroyed it. The wall was all the way down in places, and, of course, what was left of the gates had been used for firewood. Nehemiah's eyes began to fill with tears. Hanani continued by saying that honesty had gone out the window. People were not attending the makeshift temple or following the laws. People were ripping each other off and charging high interest rates. But the worst thing was that Sanballat and Tobiah were out of control. Sanballat was the Persian-appointed governor of Samaria, and Tobiah likewise was governor of Ammon. Both of these politicos claimed to be members of the Jewish faith, and both enjoyed considerable political power in Judah. "It's a shame what's going on, Nehemiah," the brothers reported. "These guys are just using our folks for more money and power. They are nothing but racketeers."

Many of our hoods are in much the same shape Judah was. Many, if not most, African American communities have taken a step back since the Civil Rights era of the fifties and sixties. My hood is typical; it's in worse shape today than ever before, with decaying empty houses and trash-covered vacant lots. The wall that once stood as a barrier against moral and physical decay, political and social injustice, has fallen. News headlines constantly report tragedy after tragedy in the community, such as drive-by shootings. There used to be a real concern for justice and safety, and we put our lives on the line for it. But today the turf is dominated by lawless dope lords, and even the police seem unwilling to challenge them, if indeed the police and drug lords are not in it together. We spend huge amounts of money to put bars on the windows and double-bolt locks on our doors, and we end up as prisoners in our own little homes.

There was a time when people were spit on and beaten for trying to vote, and many in the South were thrown into jail so that their community would have the right to vote. Now people in big cities, both North and South, hardly bother to know who's running for office, and the vote once prized so highly is not even exercised. Or if it is, it may be bought or bargained for.

Today, in many of our communities, the walls have decayed and the gate has burned. We, too, have been hit with some bad news. It is not safe to walk alone on the street, and parents have an awesome task trying to raise children with character. Crack houses are everywhere, and people feel driven to vice when there are no honest jobs available.

I knew a young girl, Pearly, who was practically on her own from age eleven. Her mother was a crackhead and all but abandoned her, also giving her baby sister away to a stranger. Pearly would pass her mother on the streets and watch her make just any arrangement in order to get a hit of crack. In order to survive, Pearly finally joined a gang. The initiation rites left her pregnant and infected with HIV. The community's heart was saddened. An overwhelming sense of guilt and concern swept through like a tidal wave. But the condition of the community had so deteriorated that even though there were churches, it seemed, on every corner, there was none with the will or the resources to come to the rescue. The community's few sincere leaders felt helpless against the tide of affairs and mourned for a way out.

Nehemiah, too, was deeply concerned and upset about his people. He had been hit with some bad news. He felt despair and grief. His heart bled for his fellow Jews, because they were in such a depressed condition. The pain he felt ran deep. He thought about how defenseless the people were without a wall and gate, and with such lawless politicians wielding such great influence. He mourned for four months with utmost sincerity, and prayed and fasted about his people's bleak situation. He asked that he might be successful as he approached the king regarding his plan to come to the aid of the folks in his hometown, Jerusalem.

He had wondered how he was going to ask the king to grant him leave and materials without seeming disloyal. But as time passed, King Artaxerxes noticed that Nehemiah's usual smile was gone. Nehemiah looked depressed. His grooming was poor. He was no longer the charming chatter box that the king knew. King Artaxerxes asked him what was going on. Nehemiah was not so depressed that he would not take advantage of the king's attention. He told the king that he was grief stricken about the graves of his ancestors and the city in general. The people were defenseless and corruption had taken over.

When the king wanted to know what he needed in time and materials, Nehemiah was fully prepared to describe the plans and material he would need to rebuild the wall and gate and to bring back order to the city. The king willingly granted Nehemiah's wishes and went so far as to make him governor of Judah, giving him papers of safe passage through the intervening territory and requisitions for the necessary lumber and other materials.

Nehemiah had prayed and meditated about what should happen once he got to the city, so he had a strategic plan. He first attended to his family's affairs. Then he investigated and became familiar with the situation in general in Jerusalem, checking out the political and religious atmosphere. Nehemiah decided that he did not want to draw attention to himself, because he did not want any opposition. He knew that Sanballat and Tobiah had allies in the city who would follow him and report his every movement. So he used care and traveled at night. He had a few good men who accompanied him. He inspected the wall in great detail. He left the city through the Valley Gate. He then went on to the Dung Gate and down toward Dragon Spring. He continued his course and ended up at the Spring Gate and passed onto the King's Pool and down to the Kidron Valley. He did a thorough survey.

In the African American community, the Million Man March would never have taken place if there had not been both deep concern and a great strategic plan. It was carefully carried out, just like the plan of the march on Washington in the 1960s, when the most people in the history of the country gathered together to put an end to injustice. Months of planning were carried out in both instances. Peace and unity took center stage.

Now when Nehemiah had completed his inspection, he shared his plan with fellow Jews. He presented it from the perspective of each family's own circumstances and the impact it had on them. They were asked to accept responsibility for the part of the wall closest to home. The group quickly identified with Nehemiah's plan and with the pain he felt about the state of the wall and the declining moral status of the community. After his presentation, he announced that he too would help to rebuild the wall. Nehemiah had won the hearts of his comrades.

There was a lot of work to be done to complete the gate. He mobilized the people of the community to join together and work smoothly. He called upon the priests, the goldsmiths, the perfumers, various merchants, the women, other segments of the community, and their leaders. Some people took on double duty because they had a real commitment.

In the African American community, there has been a call for our men to pray, seek guidance, and return to moral righteousness and restoration. This same principle must be transferred to the entire community of men, women, boys, and girls. This call is suggestive of the Million Man March. A million men and boys assembled together from all over the country to begin to get control of their lives and communities. As far as the eye could see on the mall in Washington, men and boys were praying for unity and guidance, just as Nehemiah did. Likewise, one of the great things about the march was that a tremendous amount of prayer went on prior to it. It matters not who called the march. It *does* matter that the African American community prayed for direction. And this is always essential.

Getting back to Nehemiah, the people had in him a dynamic leader, and they had a desire to restore the wall. But even with all that, there was strong opposition. The people were ridiculed and faced terroristic threats. The high priest's own son was married to Sanballat's daughter. Many of the self-styled upper class had close ties with the deeply entrenched power brokers, Sanballat and Tobiah. Nehemiah's response to this was prayer, faith, and practicality. A guard system was set up to watch out for those who were in opposition to the rebuilding of the wall. There were people on duty around the clock to ensure that the work on the wall was not interrupted.

Nehemiah and the majority of ordinary folks worked very hard to get the wall rebuilt. But he also had to counter attacks from those against rebuilding the wall. He had to arrange to buy back those who had lost all and been sold as slaves. He had to lend money and food to the poor and confront rich Jews who were ripping people off by charging high interest rates and selling slaves to foreigners. With all this and supervising the rebuilding of the wall, Nehemiah had his hands full.

Nehemiah successfully brought an end to the corruption he was faced with, but there was no rest. As the wall drew near to completion, the opposition became increasingly nervous, because all their tactics failed to stop progress on the wall. They decided that the only way to stop the work was to get rid of Nehemiah. Nehemiah's enemies tried to lure him away from the city under the pretense of holding talks. But he refused, as he said, to come down off the wall, and the talks idea did not work. So then they resorted to blackmail; he was accused of disloyalty to the emperor of Persia. That didn't work either. The final thing they tried to do was to scare or intimidate him. But Nehemiah would not be bullied. Nothing they did could shake him from his God-given task. Nehemiah continued to keep himself focused on the task. The wall was completed in less than two months. His opponents even had to admit that completion of the wall in such a short time had to be God-led and inspired.

During the 1960s, the African American community's civil rights efforts were faced with much opposition. But there was a young pastor in Cleveland who had a deep concern for what was right. He would march and protest whenever he could. He was at one particular demonstration where the civil rights workers had banded together with arms linked. In order to break up the peaceful demonstration, those in opposition brought in bulldozers to push the protesters out. The group tightened their grip and stood firm. The bulldozers continued to move forward, and they did not stop until a Catholic priest was mowed down. It did not matter what the opposition did, the protestors continued to protest. They protested to the point that the opposition gave up and did not build the new school in a predominately white neighborhood but in the African American community that needed a new school much more, where the school was overcrowded and the books were falling apart. The African American community got a new school, furnished with new equipment and books.

All is never lost—not in Jerusalem, not in Cleveland, and not in any hood anywhere—if the people have a mind to work and are willing to challenge corrupt systems. Dedicated people who stick together, who pray and plan well, and who refuse to be bought off by entrenched corruption can be sure that God blesses the effort. It may be that we have too long preached this "mind to work" text without all the realistic complications mentioned here, but the wall can be built, and the people's welfare can still be protected.

I can see the masses of Jerusalem's citizens now, all the more jubilant because they know that with God's help, they have overcome the enemy both within and without. They are shouting in the streets and carrying Nehemiah on their shoulders. They are so grateful that he used his high position on their behalf and didn't chicken out when Sanballat and Tobiah turned up the heat. They didn't say it that way, but they were overjoyed that he was such a careful planner and didn't let the restoration stop just with plans. He was a man of forthright action.

I can hear their shouts of hallelujah, so glad they can feel safer and can rear their children in peace. They are overjoyed that the back of the corrupt machine has been broken, and so happy that none of them played turncoat and accepted the bribes offered. Jerusalem may yet be the Holy City after all. Amen!

Question: The Christian church's detractors have accused it of money grubbing ever since the days of the apostle Paul. And certainly some are guilty of such sin. But is it possible to give too much, unsolicited and from the heart, to the Lord and his authentic work?

Why This Waste?

Linda Boston

Pericope: Matthew 26:6-13

When Jesus understood it, he said unto them, "Why trouble ye the woman? for she hath wrought a good work upon me" (Matthew 26:10). Jesus knew what they were thinking, and said, "Why are you criticizing her? For she has done a good thing to me" (Matthew 26:10 TLB).

"She has done what she could, and has anointed my body ahead of time for burial" (Mark 14:8 TLB).

Our story this morning comes halfway between Palm Sunday and Good Friday. It is Wednesday evening, and Jesus is having dinner at the home of Simon the leper in Bethany. We wish we could know who this Simon was and what was his condition. It is pretty clear that whatever kind of benign or malignant leprosy he had, it was gone, or more likely *he* was gone, deceased. Although he is not mentioned in the story, his house still bears his name. The scriptural evidence seems to indicate that Simon the leper was a relative or close friend, perhaps even the deceased father, of Mary, Martha, and Lazarus. The Gospel of John says this dinner was given by Mary and

Martha in the family residence in honor of Jesus' raising of Lazarus from the dead. What a cause for celebration!

Although this starts out as a typical dinner party, no doubt dreamed up and cooked by the queen of that kitchen, Sister Martha, it is a momentous occasion. The official guest of honor is Jesus, and with him are his disciples, but many of the curious and uninvited have also gathered around. I have no idea exactly how many other folks are eating, or how many are just looking or gawking at Lazarus. It's hard to tell in such a crowded little room. At any rate, we could hardly call these onlookers guests. Matthew and Mark imply that one of these "unguests" is a woman, a rank stranger to this household. They don't even know her name. She is just part of the crowd that has converged on this home, interested more in seeing the man who was raised from the dead than the man who raised him.

Suddenly all with a clear view of the scene are amazed to see the woman edge through the crowd and approach Jesus. She kneels before him. She is pouring a whole alabaster flask of very expensive spikenard perfume over Jesus' head. This is downright shocking! I mean, here is an unattached woman out in public, counter to all customs. She enters the home of Simon the leper, where there is a gathering of men, and she is unescorted, uninvited, and unannounced. She enters without ceremony, without offering a greeting of any kind to the hostess, and makes her way through the crowd to the table where Jesus is reclining. She just shows up and, without asking who is in charge, moves on to the guest of honor and breaks open a beautiful box of perfume and pours it over Jesus' head.

Can you imagine how shocking this must have been? Think about how you would feel if some strange woman came to your church unescorted, uninvited, unannounced, and without any greeting of any kind. She heads straight up the aisle and into the pulpit. While the pastor is seated and bowed in preparatory prayer, she starts pouring expensive, strong perfume all over his head. And the next thing you know, the whole church is smelling like perfume, and prayer time is over.

You know how we would whisper and carry on, and of course the ushers or security committee would advance on her and almost drag her from the sanctuary, if necessary. "She must be out of her mind, or something," we would say.

Well, the folks at Simon's house are no different. When the disciples see this woman acting like this, they are downright indignant. The first question on their minds is, "Why this waste? For what purpose have you wasted this expensive ointment?"

There was probably another question in their heads, too, the same question that was in the mind of a Pharisee when a similar thing happened in his house. Luke (7:36-50) says Jesus read the Pharisee's mind as the Pharisee wondered, "If Jesus were a real prophet, he would know what kind of a woman this is. He'd never let an embarrassing thing like this happen, or at least he wouldn't let it continue. He'd stop her."

But whatever their objections, they all miss the point. They say, "This perfume could have been sold at a high price in the market-place and the money given to the poor." They are not really that concerned about the poor, though, especially not Judas. Jesus' entire ministry has placed strong emphasis on ministry to the poor and oppressed, but the disciples are thinking the outrage of this moment will sway Jesus to condemn the woman's extravagant act. But they forget two things: First, this woman is probably from among the oppressed, and second, she also needs to be ministered to. If Jesus joins in criticizing her, she will be crushed. It would be a cruel rejection of what she feels is the very best she has to offer her Lord.

In this new follower's world, the spiritual is more important than the material. It is more important to concentrate on service to Christ and to let all other service flow out from that devotion. To deal with the poor apart from devotion to Christ can easily become merely a means of quieting one's conscience. It can be the fruit of a mind that thinks money can solve anything and control anybody.

To be sure, the poor are a large share of our Lord's ministry, but they are not all. And there are many ways to minister to the poor. So Jesus says, "Leave her alone! Why are you bothering this woman? She has done a beautiful thing to me. You'll always have some poor folks around, but you won't always have me. When she poured this perfume on my body, she did it to prepare me ahead of time for burial. And she will always be remembered for this deed. The story of what she has done will be told throughout the whole world in memory of her."

Before I go too far, I had better quit signifying too strongly about these guests. Jesus' own disciples are among them. In fact, they are the first ones mentioned as getting indignant and calling the woman's actions a waste. I suspect we all need to see just how much we too are indignant, like these disciples on whom Jesus is depending. These men are good people, but they are made uncomfortable by this woman's all-out devotion. Something down deep in them may sense her act as a judgment against their own level of devotion.

The first bit of good news in this account is that the life stories of the disciples do not end here. The disciples grow and grow and grow. And the day comes in the life of almost all of them when their devotion and obedience to the Lord lead them to even greater levels of sacrifice. They actually give not perfume but their blood—their very lives. And we here have the same potential for growing in Christ and increasing in our devotion and obedience.

Let's go back to the woman, though. There's more we don't know about her: Where did she come from? And how did she get this expensive perfume in the first place? It could have been worth as much as a whole year's wages, if she were a peasant. But however she got the perfume, and however intelligent she is or is not, she has her mind on a single, important focus. She has the awesome integrity of soul to pour out the best she has for her Lord. There is none of this stuff we call half-stepping. She is all-out devoted.

She is so completely devoted that she does some amazingly courageous and audacious things. Real courage is not ignorant of penalties, but it is willing to pay the price after having counted the cost. This woman has the courage to trespass against a few major traditions or laws, and suffer the consequences if need be. She apparently takes no inventory of who is in the house. She doesn't ask anyone who is in charge or with whom she should speak to get clearance. She could easily be arrested for trespassing. She has no idea that Jesus could or would ask the disciples to back off. All she knows is that Jesus means enough to her for it to be worth even getting arrested, just to try to be near him and honor him in the way she is moved to do. The woman just acts according to her deep intuition, and that's that. This takes courage! Great courage!

Can you imagine yourself ever dreaming of such a courageous deed, much less doing it? You have to be either crazy, extremely fanatical, or so full of devotion that it overrides all common sense and drives you to reckless firmness of purpose.

This woman's determination arouses yet another question. What kind of person ever dreams up such a demonstration? If you have never tried to depart from tradition, you ought to give it serious consideration some time. I can see this unnamed woman looking at a horrified audience and feeling really good about what she has done. She doesn't smirk or act disrespectful of the crowd, but down deep she is saying, "I did it. I did it. I did just what I said I was going to do."

A famous theologian named Paul Tillich said that real living or real being is not a matter of what you have. It's a matter of deciding what you want to do and just doing it. This is being. Everything else is non-being. If we translate Tillich into street talk, he would say, "No matter how much you got, if you can't decide what you really wanna do and say you gonna do it, and then do it, you ain't got whatcha need." This woman's determined act asserts her selfhood—her being—in a way that offers life's greatest satisfaction and fulfillment.

However respectable or religious Martha's room full of horrified guests may be, and however proper they are according to the law, none of them is likely ever to have so deep a satisfaction as this woman has. To be is to say for yourself what you will do and then making it happen. Some of us spend all of our lives letting somebody else determine goals for us. But God, who made us in God's own image, made us for the purpose of being—for making moral decisions, for creative decision making under God and for ourselves.

One more word about this sister. She gets even more out of her courageous deed than the deep joy of asserting her being, the satisfaction of celebrating her indomitable personhood. You will remember that she hears her Lord raise his voice above the assembly and shout, "Leave her alone! You may not understand what she is doing and why. But I am fully aware of what she's up to. She is doing for me what I may not get at the proper time on my way to my grave. Neither my enemies nor my friends may have a chance to anoint me according to our ways, when I am taken away and crucified. But she has anointed me before time. I think that's beautiful."

Listen, as our Lord continues, "She has done what she could. She has offered the best she knew to offer from inside the limitations of her life. She has made it plain that nothing she has is too precious to be given away in my name. I tell you that in the years to come, what she has done shall be spoken of as a memorial to her. In the centuries ahead, untold millions will remember that I said she has done what she could."

We here this morning can't know exactly what is in this woman's mind, but Jesus applauds her and accepts her act of devotion graciously. The specific details of what is on her mind do not matter. The important thing in her thinking is that Jesus deserves her most precious possession. In her value system, nothing is too good for Jesus.

I'd love to know what is going on in this woman's mind. But here is the second bit of good news in this story: I can hear Jesus say the same thing to me, too, if I love and serve the Lord the way the woman with the alabaster flask did. Jesus is telling all of us, "There is no waste in sincere devotion. All I ever ask of anybody is their very best. And when you do what you can for me—for my sake, for my causes, for my kingdom—then your work will also be remembered, and it will last."

Question: Is our task as preachers one of lofty, learned discourse? Or is the knowledge of the Word only the beginning of vocation in which our most important communication is our living of the Word, in the pulpit and out?

Being the Word

Elizabeth Mitchell Clement

Pericope: 2 Timothy 2:8-15

Do your best to present yourself to God as one approved by God, . . . rightly explaining the word of truth (2 Timothy 2:15 NRSV).

Take good care to stand before God on account of whose grace (before the world began) and according to whose purposes we have a holy calling . . . to (figuratively) lay open the divine message (2 Timothy 2:15, author's translation).

Paul has gotten wind that Timothy is having trouble in his church. Students of church administration will note that the problem in the church is addressed to the leadership, not the whole congregation. As important as his churches surely are to Paul, here he is the master pastor speaking to the very personal need of his "dearly beloved son" in ministry. Paul's solution is to lay his hands on Timothy by letter, in words that remind him of the "form of sound words" (2 Timothy 1:13), "the standard of sound teaching" (NRSV) that he has learned from Paul himself.

The cause of Tim's tears is "wrangling over words" or striving about words to no profit (2:14), and Paul has a clear word about such an enterprise: No. Nein! Ix-nay. Avoid it. "Not only is it a worthless enterprise," he says. "It's a subversive occupation."

These are hard words for seminary-trained people. We see a lot of words on any given day. How many times have my children asked, "Mom, are you going to read *all* day? How long does it take to write a sermon?" Paul tells Timothy his time can be better spent.

OK. But if not words, then what? The King James Version answers, "Study to show yourself approved" (v. 15). I'm sorry, Paul, I thought I just heard you say that striving about words was a waste of time? The New Revised Standard Version is no more helpful: "Do your best to present yourself as one approved by God."

Perhaps Timothy's problem was not the same as ours. Timothy surely did not have a dozen different translations to navigate. In fact, Timothy probably didn't have a whole lot of documents of any kind, not a lot of words on paper. (Somehow, he had made it to full-fledged ministry with no books!)

Of course, it isn't that Timothy is without training altogether. Not at all. It seems likely that, because his father was Greek, Timothy was educated in the classics. We also know that he was not without home training; his mother and his grandmother had seen to that. Paul has no doubt about the young man's qualification for ministry; he has himself "trained him up in the way he should go." Timothy is Paul's protege, maybe even a prodigy. Tim is Paul's "boy"! (I think that's a man thing.)

So, in a very real sense, Timothy's preparation has not been a study of words but a study of lives. Timothy has studied his mother and his grandmother. Timothy has lived with Paul—the preacher, apostle, and teacher—in Corinth, Ephesus, and all around the diaspora, "in season and out of season" (4:2). Timothy has been a diligent and attentive student, not of the clever abstractions, not of the verbal jousting of one great scholar against another. Timothy has studied the lives of the faithful. And Paul wants him to remember these standards, not the words that may describe them.

"Remember Jesus Christ," he says. "You know, Joseph's boy,

David's great-great-great-great-grandson. You remember him. He lived not too far from here, not too long ago. That's my gospel. You see, Timmy, to 'rightly divide the word of truth' (2:15), you have to *be* the gospel."

Luke Johnson (*Writings of the New Testament*) says Paul is writing this letter to remind Timothy of the models of faith he has had, and that he is himself the reminder for the assembly. Johnson calls 2 Timothy a "personal parenetic letter," a classical genre of the period. In contemporary genre it is a "you-see-Timmy." You've never heard of a "you-see-Timmy"? The television series "Lassie" used to come on every Sunday evening. (Some of you can remember back that far. That was the half hour of television we were allowed to watch for the week.) At the end of each heart-wrenching episode, Timmy's mother or grandfather would put an arm around the boy and put the whole story in perspective. "You see, Timmy, ..."

Paul has not sent a letter as we usually understand it. These are not just words Paul puts on a page and sends to help his young friend. In their world, Paul's letter to Timothy bears Paul's presence—his person—to the distant place. So by his letter, Paul lays on his hands—puts an arm around Timothy—and puts the whole ugly business in perspective.

"You see, Timmy, your ministry is to rightly divide the word of truth." Of course, Timothy wants to know what we want to know: Exactly how is the word of truth "rightly divided"? We might not like Paul's answer. In the final analysis, he seems to me to respond in very much the way one of the desert fathers of the fourth century does. When Abba Pambo was asked to say an edifying word to a visiting archbishop, he replied, "If he is not edified by my silence, he will not be edified by my speech."

"You see, Timmy, the right explanation of the word of truth is not in talking the talk but in walking the walk. To rightly divide the word of truth with your people, you have to *be* the word of truth. That is the form of teaching you have learned. That's why you believe it so firmly. Hold fast to that. Be reminded of that and remind the others. Focus your being, son. In your person will they be reminded of the truth."

But what is the word of truth? Whatever it is, Paul is saying it will not be found by spending more time in the pastor's study. Paul has never said that a person is approved by God because she has worked hard. No, in his greeting in this very letter, he brings to remembrance the "holy calling, not according to our works, but according to God's own purpose and grace, which was given us in Christ Jesus before the world began" (1:9). So what does Paul mean?

"You see, Timmy, you must take great care as you stand before God on account of whose grace (before the world began) and according to whose purposes we are called. Take great care to lay open the divine message, so that in you, it is seen, and so that by your gracious presence, the grace of God may be known. That's what it means to show yourself approved to God.

"You see, Timmy, we have been approved by God, before the world began, and called according to the purposes of God. Stay away from the word wars. You don't have time. You are too busy shouting about that blessed assurance and praising our Savior all the day long. Do that work, Timothy, and you'll never have to be ashamed.

"Take great care, Timmy, to stand up and to stand out like one who knows how good God is. In your life will the word of truth come alive. It'll be all over you, everywhere you go. Take it to the whole world. 'Do the work of an evangelist, carry out your ministry fully' (4:5 NRSV).

"You see, Timmy, that's what I have tried to do. I have been poured out as a libation. But I won't be here always. You see, Timmy, that day will come when I present myself to God as one finally approved. I want to hear God say, 'You have fought the good fight, you have finished the race, you have kept and lived the faith. There is reserved for you a crown in the realm of my righteousness, which I will gladly give you. And not only you, but all who look forward to my coming and the kingdom's.'"

Question: Dare Christians of the highest principles fail to relate closely to those of lower standards, and thus bypass opportunities to love and accept them into higher self-esteem and higher (Christian) principles of living?

The Day Samaritan Sally Met Jesus

Beletia Marvray Diamond

Pericope: John 4:1-42

Come, see a man, which told me all things that ever I did: is not this the Christ? (John 4:29 NRSV).

The two ushers at the door were quite proper, both in their dress and their decorum. They smiled graciously as the members moved from the landing at the top of the steps and advanced through the great oak doors. Then suddenly their countenances changed. The "tin grin" of welcome faded a bit as they moved from the side to the center of the opening. They were still trying to smile, but their words said something else. Standing before them was a poorly dressed woman of perhaps forty years. Her hair was unkempt, her eyes were reddish, and her walk just a wee bit unsteady. "Good morning," they said. "We're happy to see you! However, we're sure you'll be more comfortable here another day, when you've had time to really get yourself ready for church."

The woman could find no words to respond, so she withdrew

silently and sheepishly, with bowed head and crushed heart. Would she always and ever be rejected as one of the dregs of humanity? It had seemed so ever since she lost that first job for coming to work high almost twenty years ago. For their part, the ushers felt they had handled a delicate matter with diplomacy. After all, the church of Jesus Christ demands respect. And it was their responsibility to maintain high levels of dignity in worship. Unbathed, intoxicated people were a disgrace, and they must "clean up their act a bit" if they wanted to be received in God's house.

Granted, standards are important. But are there other concerns of equal or greater importance? Is the church exclusively a gathering of the spiritually and morally elite, the healthy and whole, oh yes, and those who are plainly within reach of these standards? Or is the church a hospital and hostel for those who are hurting and lost? Whether the derelicts live in plush, high-rise town houses or the gutters of the so-called hood, is there a sense in which we Christians are called to a ministry of respect for the least and last, the most unrespectable people of our time and place? Or is it more effective to take a stand and make people earn their respect before they can be received into our community? Jesus' ministry offers some interesting and challenging views on the question.

Come with me to the site of a well in Samaria, and meet a woman of low-to-no respect. Her name is Sally, a sun-kissed, brown-skinned woman whom we find trudging along the dry, dusty road of her village on her way to draw water from the public well. It is high noon on a day much like here in Georgia in the month of July. The rays of the sun seem to be the most intense, extremely hot, without so much as a hint of a breeze blowing anywhere. With a water pitcher on her shoulder, she is wearing an ankle-length, loose-fitting, faded blue, cotton dress that caresses her once voluptuous body. To keep the direct rays of the sun from burning down upon her head, she is wearing a lightweight, flowing headdress, which outlines a face that was once striking and attractive. Is Samaritan Sally a reaper of what she has sown? Or is she a victim of situations and circumstances over which she has had no control? Or is it some of both? Whatever, Samaritan Sally is on her way to draw water from the well, for her household.

Of course, we have to wonder why she comes at this hour of the day, rather than in the cool of the evening, as is the custom. That's when the other women of the city make this journey. Doesn't she know that if she came in the evening, she could share in the girl-talk with them? After all, they've been busy in their homes all day long, and they are eagerly looking forward to their daily chance to exhale. They can hardly wait to free themselves of the constraints their culture places on women, to vent some of their frustrations as wives and mothers, concerns that can only be shared with those with like experiences.

Oops! How thoughtless of me! Of course, she knows all about the chatter at the well. That's precisely why she doesn't go when the rest of them are there. They shall not have any more opportunities to make her feel like dirt. It's downright cruel, the way they ostracize her because of her past. They just assume she is without high morals and values, one who can't be trusted alone with their husbands or even their sons, one to be avoided at all costs. She has no choice but to come at this hour of the day to avoid their holier-than-thou attitudes, their gossipy conversations, and yes, even their glaring stares.

Well, on this same road travels a tall, slender, sun-kissed, dark-skinned, gentle-faced young man. It's Joseph and Mary's son, Jesus, and some of his disciples. They look tired and weary. Perspiration is dripping from their foreheads. Where are they coming from? Where are they going? They must be on their way to Galilee from Judea, although people don't usually take this shorter route.

I expect they'll stop for a bit of refreshment there by the well. Yes, they've decided to stop for a bit, but it looks as if the disciples are going on, leaving Jesus alone at the well. Yes, I see, they're hungry. They're leaving Jesus at the well while they go to town to buy some food.

"Alone at last, for a few moments," thinks Jesus, as he sits beside the well. He gazes out into the distance, attempting to unwind from his long journey, wiping the perspiration from his brow, shaking the dust from his feet. He longs for a moment of tranquility, but he can't help reflecting on the hostile relationship that exists between the Jews and Samaritans, the traditional hatred that arose between them when they were separated by the exile. "Why can't they love one another, in spite of their differences?" he ponders. That's one reason why he felt he needed to go through Samaria.

Suddenly he is distracted from his thoughts by the sound of footsteps. The silence is broken as someone intrudes on his solitude. Here stands Samaritan Sally, getting ready to draw water from the well to fill her pitcher. Looking at her, he sees a wounded soul who has been stripped of any fulfillment whatever in life. Compassion, coupled with his concern for a drink of cool water, becomes the order of the day for him.

"Sally," he says to her, "would you be so kind as to give me a drink of water?" Just imagine him speaking to her! This is definitely a no-no in this culture, for a man to be seen talking in public with a woman who is not his wife. (Now perhaps there are opportunities when sneak conversations between males and females occur, but never does a man or a woman dare to be so bold as to openly defy custom this way.) Obviously this Jesus does not let tradition stand in the way when there is need. Of course, Jesus is not your everyday Joe. He's a gentleman in every sense of the imagination, never demanding or overly aggressive, never manipulative. Still, he is one who always goes against the grain of religiosity. He often speaks of ecclesiastical dignitaries as whitened sepulchers, full of dead mens' bones.

With Jesus, I guess you could say that each of us is special. With him, each of us has a name, and he always calls people by their names. Sally is startled that he knows her name and equally surprised by his boldness to speak to her in public. She looks into his eyes and can't help smiling, even though she doesn't open up right away. She no longer feels inferior; her inhibitions about who she is in the sight of others don't seem to matter any more. Her being seen talking to this man doesn't bother her either; it is swallowed up into the thickness of the sweltering heat. She actually gets involved in quite a conversation.

The question of racial interaction is of great concern for her: "How is that you, a Jew, ask a drink of me, a woman of Samaria?" (John 4:9 NRSV). (Listen to her, becoming bold and confident.) She knows very well that Jews have no dealings with Samaritans. His reply to her is even more astounding. "If you knew the gift of God, and who it is that is saying to you, 'Give me to drink,' you would have asked him, and he would have been given you living water. Those who drink of the water that I will give will never be thirsty. The water that I will give will become in them a spring of water gushing up to eternal life" (vv. 13-14 NRSV). This causes Sally some concern. The only water she knows about is the water that flows freely from the springs. But she carries on, asking for some of this water that will spare her the job of walking to the well.

She keeps this illegal conversation going, and she gazes at him unashamedly. "It's something about this man," she ponders. "I feel comfortable in his presence. It doesn't seem to matter to him that he is breaking the law by talking to me. It's pleasant to have someone to talk to. So why not keep this going and ask for some of this water?" For her as an outcast in her community, the decision to ask for what he offers is a way at least to keep this rare conversation going.

Jesus replies, "Go, get your husband and I'll tell both of you about this water."

Bam! "There it is," she thinks. "He'll know all about me, and then he'll send me away and have nothing more to say to me." She lowers her gaze and drops her head in shame, as has become her custom, and replies, "Sir, I have no husband."

"You're absolutely correct, Sally," he gently replies. "You've had five husbands, and the man you're now living with is not your husband." It's quite clear that Jesus is not one for playing games. He calls the shots as they are, and truth sets us free.

Sally waits, bracing herself to hear the concluding words of condemnation flung toward her. She slowly raises her head and looks again into his eyes, which are calm and serene, even though they are penetrating, appearing to see into her very soul. With her heart racing, her thoughts swirling, she thinks, "This must be a man of God. How could he know these things about me and not condemn me? How could he know these things about me and not be ashamed to be seen talking to me? My neighbors know about me and my struggles, and they're always putting me down, as if they're better than me. Acting as if they've never done anything wrong, they shun me and refuse to be seen talking to me. Who is this man?"

Stirred by his continued interest in her, she risks pursuing the conversation and lets him know unabashedly that she thinks he must be a prophet. Then she raises a question about religion, and finally she confesses that she believes that some day, the Messiah will come and reveal all things. Jesus decides that he might as well confide in her and let her know who he really is. "I that speak to you am he," he says.

About that time the disciples come back. They can't get over the fact that he is talking with this woman. They ask him point blank, "Why are you talking with her?" But that doesn't bother her now. Speechless, excited, relieved, yet greatly astonished, she knows without a doubt that she has met an emissary from heaven. And heaven respects and accepts her, even if the town of Sychar doesn't.

What joy! What joy she feels! She leaves her waterpot at the well and runs to tell her neighbors, "Come see a man who told me everything I have ever done. Come see a man who doesn't condemn me. He treats me like a human being, yes, a child of God. Come see a man whom I believe with all of my heart is the Christ, the Son of the living God."

So what happened the day Samaritan Sally met Jesus the Christ? Sally's life was instantly changed. Sally looked into the eyes of Jesus and knew that she was truly loved and accepted and respected as a person. It was not a selfish or demanding love, nor a lustful or a manipulative love. She was loved with the pure and undefiled love of God. Suddenly she was a new person in her own mind as well as in the mind of Christ. And she wasted no time living up to that new vision of herself as a child of God.

The outcasts and down-and-outers of our world still need to be respected and loved into the people God made them to be. And there are still people here and there who follow the path of Christ by breaking with the traditions of so-called respectability, and by offering love and respect to unfortunate derelicts.

Just yesterday, as Negro History Month was drawing to a close, the local newspaper ran a half-page article and picture with the headline, "Businessman's faith puts former down-and-outers on different path." Pictured was a forty-one-year-old man who had been released from a drug treatment program only four years ago. An investment broker with a previous history of alcoholism and a heart of love found and respected this former addict, and today they have two thrift store ministries, helping hundreds, maybe thousands, with life's necessities. And they have already trained and moved to employment some forty-five homeless and formerly addicted people. All this program does is surround the people with contagious respect for self and unconditional love— and, of course, a chance to earn a decent wage.

That's mostly what happened to Sally. Once her crushed spirit and low opinion of herself were impacted, her nerve was awesome. She hadn't changed clothing nor received any material advantage as such. She just met Jesus, who helped her change her mind about Sally. Jesus blessed her spirit with his unconditional love and willingness to be associated with her, and that bred self-respect. We could say Jesus held a crown over her head, and she did her best to live up to it—without knowing that she was trying, she was so happy.

And Sally made major history. No matter how many thousands or even millions go forth to preach the lordship of Christ, the first one to say it abroad in public was Sally. Yes, those dear gossipers at the well have something to talk about now for sure. The love and hope they failed to offer was supplied by our Lord Jesus

Christ, and Sally is *somebody* for the records of the world. She could be called the first preacher—yes, a woman, and yes, a person with a questionable personal history, and yes, a woman in a culture dead set on keeping her down. But the love and simple respect of Jesus touched her and made her whole. Hallelujah!

Question: Contemporary American Christianity tends to reject and ridicule old-fashioned fire and brimstone, or fearful faithfulness. And rightly so. Emphasis now is placed on a positive gospel. But have we gone too far? Is it possible to enjoy abundant life and still be sternly alert and prepared to deal with the needs and evils of the real world?

At Ease in Zion

Emilygail Richardson Dill

Pericopes: Amos 6:1-7; Matthew 26:36-46

Woe to them that are at ease in Zion, and trust in the mountain of Samaria (Amos 6:1 NRSV).

Watch and pray, that you enter not into temptation: the spirit indeed is willing, but the flesh is weak (Matthew 26:41 NRSV).

When I was a child, my father would take us down to the Warwick Camp, the military training site in my country, to watch the Bermuda Regiment soldiers-in-training. I would look forward to these opportunities and watch closely the commanding officer as he shouted out the orders to the troops. Of course, when we got home and were playing around the house, we created a game called "army." One of us would assume the role of the commanding officer. That individual would shout out, "Pattoon shun-i-an!" or some other unintelligible phrase, and the others would all scramble as we attempted to reenact the positions we had seen the soldiers assume.

I never did quite figure out just what that individual was saying or what we were supposed to do. The one command I did recognize, however, was the injunction to be "at ease." This was the time when the soldiers were allowed to assume a relaxed position, while still remaining silent and staying in place. This point in our game and in the exercises of the soldiers was a time all looked forward to. We could let down our guard just a bit and free our minds for a time. We waited expectantly for the command, "At ease!"

Spiritually and morally speaking, a great many of us are at ease. We have assumed a relaxed position. We remain silent, even though we are yet in our proper places. But although the at-ease position is one of comfort and low stress, it can be dangerous. Children playing at army games and soldiers engaged in mere practice exercises can at some point assume the at-ease position without risk. But we, as children of God and soldiers in the army of our righteous Lord, must take care never to assume this risky position. We must never be tricked into believing that we can let down our guard without fear of attack by our enemy, Satan. When we are at ease, we drop our guard. We become vulnerable, creating an easy target for the enemy to come in and destroy our position. The reality is that in the life of a committed Christian, we never hear the command to be "at ease."

Today's Scripture lesson begins with the statement, "Woe to them that are at ease in Zion," meaning that great sorrow, grief, and misery will befall those that are at ease in Zion. This mount was a choice dwelling place. The inhabitants were both honored and protected by living there. They believed that God's residence was there also, so they were close to Jehovah and safe from divine judgment and enemies, as well. They believed that dwelling in Zion was enough. Those that dwelt on the mountain of Samaria were equally proud, for they too had a direct relationship to Israel and her God. The mountain of Samaria was the capital of a powerful region and a main center of religion.

Amos, however, warns the people not to become complacent because of their standing in church and society. He even specifically names other kingdoms and reminds the people of the fact that those kingdoms met their ruin. He tells the people to go and look at Calneh, a great city built by Nimrod, which is now in ruins. From there he tells them to go look at Hamath, one of the great cities of Syria, and also Gath. All of these cities were larger and more prosperous than Zion and Mount Samaria, yet they had been destroyed. These city-kingdoms had ample reason to believe they could assume an at-ease position, because of their wealth and prosperity. Yet, because of that very assumption, they met destruction.

As I continued to read Amos's warning to the people, I could not help but note the similarities between the people and communities of Amos's time and ours. We become satisfied and take our rest. We have reached a certain level of affluence and decided that we no longer need to be partakers in the moral and spiritual war that is raging around us. We sit back and reflect on the progress we have made as a people, and we decide to be at ease. We smile proudly when we listen to the statistics that positively reflect our minority-within-the-minority's strides toward middle-class status, and we consciously ignore reports that disclose the fact that although some of us have come a long, long way, our people as a whole have a long, long way to go.

We go out to our jobs daily and wait impatiently for the hour when we can leave this place of labor and retreat to our lovely homes, where we can be at ease. We block out the images of the dope addicts, prostitutes, and homeless children for fear that they will create nightmares that will destroy our rest and "mess with" our at-ease positions. We turn up our noses at people with AIDS and silently veto efforts to provide adequate hospitalization and support for them, especially if services are provided in our neighborhoods. We forget that with the rapidly increasing rate of infection and the various modes of transmission, our sons, our daughters, our friends, and even ourselves might inadvertently become victims of this fatal disease. We cannot afford to be at ease!

In 1987 the World Council of Churches declared an Ecumenical Decade for Churches in Solidarity with Women. We united our voices and publicly committed our support. Yet nine years later, women within our own denominational structures are experiencing oppression as never seen before. We have seen the rate of violence against women reach astronomical proportions in our community. There are now more single-parent households headed by women than we have ever seen before in the history of our country. The crime rate throughout the land rises daily. In the face of these realities we cannot, should not, be at ease!

We choose for ourselves the finest in material possessions and busy ourselves with enjoying them to the utmost. We no longer look forward to pie in the sky, by and by. We would rather have cashmere while we're here. And please do not ask us to share. Our primary concern has become ourselves, and we blatantly ignore others.

This at-ease position is displeasing to God. We have been instructed that the strong *must* bear the infirmities of the weak, that we *must* help bear the burdens of our sisters and brothers. If that sounds like a cross and if it seems antithetical to being at ease, you heard right.

But the redemptive cross is the most fulfilling load anyone could have. No true mother would deny that babies are a load, but who would deny that it is abundant living, ease or no ease?

We cannot afford to be at ease. When the Wesleys founded this great church body, they were not at ease. When they launched a worldwide missionary movement and founded schools and hospitals, they were not at ease. When Methodists like Rosa Parks and the pastors who petitioned for the 1954 Supreme Court decision helped to launch the Civil Rights revolution, they were not at ease. Today we enjoy the fruits of their labors.

But we, like the characters in the movie *The Lion King*, have adopted an "akunamatata"-type attitude. I can't figure out whether it is out of fear, like the little lion Baby Simba in the movie, or out of sheer carelessness, but we need to get up, sacrifice ease, and make a difference.

I am reminded of Jesus' experience with the disciples in the Garden of Gethsemane (Matthew 26:36-56). Unintentionally, his closest disciples, the ones on whom the salvation of the world was to depend, had failed Jesus' request to watch while he prayed. They had yielded to ease and fallen fast asleep. It was the first of three times Jesus would return from his prayer a short distance away and find them snoring. He didn't fuss with them or get angry; he just voiced surprise. "What? Couldn't you guys watch with me for one hour?" But then in compassion he offered the best prescription there is for people who keep getting drowsy from being at ease: "Watch and pray, that ye enter not into temptation": the spirit indeed wants to be loyal and dependable, but your bodies are weak and fatigued.

But that is not the end of the story. They who were ashamed of their drowsiness, they who were chosen for this intimate last devotional time and who failed Jesus in the process, they whom Jesus treated with kind understanding—*they* moved on and lived up to the challenge of their Savior after all. When the newborn Christian church was under serious fire and their very lives were at stake, Peter forgot all about ease and stood up to the religious establishment. No longer did fatigue or ease or even his personal survival matter.

I hear a certain gusto and a deep satisfaction in his voice when he says:

> If we this day be examined because of the good deed done to this impotent man, by what means he has been made whole; be it known to every one of you, and to all the people of Israel for that matter, that by the name of Jesus Christ of Nazareth, whom you had the nerve to crucify, whom God raised from the dead, by him and his power does this man stand before you made whole and healthy. Jesus is like the keystone that the builders rejected because they didn't understand it, and it became the chief stone in the arch. And that's not all. Neither is there any salvation to be found in any other name under heaven! (Acts 4:9-12)

Their boldness awed their accusers; they finally went free.

Peter and the other disciples had watched and prayed, and they were ready for the test this time. They may have been tired, but no ease of body could compare with the joy of the spirit they felt that day. Hallelujah!

Question: Is the reconstruction of the black family and community contingent on the subordination of women to men? Or will we all be liberated together, equally?

Case Dismissed

Jacquelyn Donald-Mims

Pericope: John 7:53–8:11

Jesus straightened up and said to her, "Woman, where are they? Has no one condemned you?" (John 8:10 NRSV).

What in the world is the African American community doing to its women? They are sometimes depicted through icons of intellect and power, such as Barbara Jordan; they are seen as fearless in Harriet Tubman; they beget revolution and transformation in Rosa Parks; and they exemplify real motherhood in Clara McBride "Mother" Hale. But at the same time, they are all too often portrayed as the confused, nagging, and insecure dependents of either strong men or the welfare system.

Can we afford to lose the African American woman to the adversity imposed from within her own ethnic family, "the hood"? Dare we continue to make her weak, or shall her strength be enhanced and preserved? Examine the welfare of the world for the African American woman in the midst of constant and unnecessary physical violence and emotional condemnation. Can we afford for the African American woman to become subdued and ineffective in the world, and unable to take her part in influencing positive transformation?

A powerful and relevant story is found in the biblical account in John 7:53-8:11, in which Jesus halts a case of legalized physical abuse and execution, heaped on a defenseless woman. As Jesus rose early in the morning to teach in the churchyard, he drew a group of accusing scribes and Pharisees into an experience of profound learning and self-confrontation.

A woman stands accused by the professional men in the hood, who bring her to face their indictment of the sin of adultery. She is charged as promiscuous. These male pillars of the community have conspired to test Jesus to see if he will fall into their entrapment. Will the popular and kindly Jesus dare to fully restore this victimized woman to dignity and publicly affirm his soft attitude toward woman and sexuality? Or will he support the literal law and have her stoned, losing his great popularity? Her accusers' warped minds are intent on doing him in either way. The fact that the plan requires the fatal stoning of a woman is to them unimportant.

The woman of this Scripture passage is probably no different from today's woman—a family woman. The woman is married. Although the text does not indicate the presence of children, because there was no modern technology for contraception, we can probably assume she is a mother. She is at the very least a potential mother. Perhaps this woman is also young, vivacious, the envy of most women's eyes, and the attraction of men's eyes.

Unfortunately, there is evidence throughout most of Scripture of the great subjection and oppression of women. Immediately obvious is this woman's lowered status in society, in that she is nameless. While the scribes and Pharisees are named by their distinctive career titles, the woman is referred to only as the adulterous woman.

The woman is further disadvantaged by the inequitable cultural and religious norms of her day. For example, while the woman is brought by the scribes and Pharisees to stand before Jesus as judge, conspicuous by his absence is the man with whom the woman was caught in adultery. The Jewish law requires that both, not just one of the guilty parties of adultery, be put to death

(Deuteronomy 22:22; Leviticus 20:10). Surely it is impossible for the woman to be guilty by herself. Yet no charges are brought against the man who was the woman's partner. Surely the scribes and Pharisees caught her partner in the same act. Even though the accusers knew the man's identity, he was not identified as a sinner like the woman, nor was he threatened with death.

The accusers refused to apply the law equitably. Why? Was the adulterous man one of the "boys in the hood," one of the scribes or Pharisees? Was the guilty man somebody the accusers needed to protect? Was the male adulterer one of the big men in town, serving on the city council, county commission, or state legislature? Was he a doctor or a lawyer? Could he have been a millionaire who always paid the hush-hush money to cover up his extramarital relations? Would daring to bring him to justice jeopardize someone's prized business relationship? Was his part ignored because he was the upstanding, flawless civic citizen and society man of the day? What was going on in the minds of the accusers, that the adulterous man was protected? Meanwhile, in all legal literalness, they pursue the woman and present her for sentencing. The woman here is the sole "bad person."

I can imagine the names she might have been called by the salacious gathering of men. Think about what women today are called—"tramp," "slut," "whore," "hot," "nasty," "unfit," "flygirl," "easy," or "dirty"—and conceivably even worse. There is no consideration for the redeeming good qualities she might have. Neither is there any mention of the other activities she might have going on in her life that would suggest that her life was worth preserving. Our legal system today has been slow to enforce the protection of women, slow to define domestic violence more aggressively as a serious violation of human rights. Scripture records that this woman was condemned to violent death, and the issue of violence is still relevant today.

Back to our story, though. There is hope. As God would have it, the accusing men have brought her to the right rabbi, Jesus, to be the judge and final arbiter in the case against this woman. Jesus has the reputation of being teacher, master, healer, and the one who forgives. Divine intervention for justice is available in Jesus. Jesus becomes like the modern-day battered women's shelter for this woman. Jesus provides sanctuary for this woman who stands accused by men.

Jesus does not respond by convicting the woman, in accord with the strictures of Jewish law. Nor does he approve of her behavior. Rather, he responds in love and grace and equity. Instead of condoning her, Jesus challenges, "Let anyone among you who is without sin be the first to cast a stone at her" (John 8:7 NRSV). And Jesus teaches that in the eyes of God, the woman is the equal of the men in the hood. Just as all have sinned and fallen short of the glory of God, all can receive salvation, and become "somebody."

Jesus refuses to participate in heightening the condemnation of the woman. Rather, his action is to bend down and write on the ground. While the Scripture does not reveal exactly what Jesus wrote on the ground, we are sure that whatever Jesus wrote, it was just the right water to extinguish any fire of controversy.

Jesus marks in the ground, perhaps enumerating the sins of the woman's accusers. Jesus might have written on the ground to spell out the names of the accusing men who were themselves adulterers. Maybe Jesus wrote on the ground the name of the man caught in the act, revealing his identity.

Perhaps Jesus had some things to say about this woman, too. Maybe Jesus found the woman to be a victim of sexual harassment in the work place, with her career and livelihood in jeopardy and salvageable only through her submission to sexual demands by her powerful male employer. The woman could have been an object of manipulation for the men in the hood, because her death would conveniently remove her as a witness to the identity of her sex mate. Perhaps she was a victim of neglect and physical violence by her husband, and Jesus was encouraging her to seek a more positive and loving relationship elsewhere. Maybe she was driven to seek other remedies to her life of pain and continued physical and emotional abuse. It is possible that the woman had been a victim of rape, or incest under her overpowering father. (In any case, it is altogether unjustified to assume that she was a prostitute, any more than that her partner was a dreg of society.) Jesus wrote on the ground not only to show that the men were guilty but to show that the woman was as acceptable as they. Jesus possibly wrote, "This woman is God's beloved daughter, to whom God offers unconditional love." Maybe Jesus raised her lowly status by writing her true name and ended by calling her a true disciple. The text does not tell us why the woman was impelled to sinful action. Jesus, making no issue of it, never condones or condemns her alleged actions. Nor does he even agree that she is guilty. Jesus simply looks beyond her faults and sees her needs.

To the utmost, Jesus is a forgiving Savior. Jesus sets this captive woman free from her bloodthirsty captors. Jesus simply releases her, saying, "Go your way, and from now on do not sin again"— *case dismissed!*

Jesus' act was a demonstration of grace and love. Jesus, the just and righteous Savior, dismissed the case against the condemned woman. The happy ending for the woman also freed up her male accusers, once obsessed with violence and nullification. As the Scripture tells us, they departed, one by one. For the men as well—*case dismissed!*

Even subject to criticism himself in that culture, Jesus was the only one who would suffer with the woman and stand up in public to acknowledge who the woman was and whose she was—a child of God. Who was this woman? She was somebody! Whose was this woman? She was a child of God! Though powerless and unable to be "one of the boys," she was one of God's chosen vessels. Verses 10 and 11 (NRSV) say, "Jesus straightened up and said to her, 'Woman, where are they? Has no one condemned you? . . . Neither do I.'" *Case dismissed!* The woman is once again the virtuous and phenomenal woman in society that God intended her to be.

Question: If 11:00 A.M. on Sunday is the most segregated hour of the American week, why is this? If this is justified by the fact that people worship truly only in their own culture, and cultures reflect our unevenly blessed experience, do we have to wait until all is equal to worship together? Or can we let Jesus bulldoze away the rubble of old traditions and free us inside the black church from the bonds of classism, racism, colorism, sexism, and me-ism?

Gentle Jesus: Bulldozer

Lillian Frier-Webb

Pericope: John 4:3-30

[Jesus] had to go through Samaria (John 4:4 NRSV).

A common sight in the Old City of Jerusalem is the yellow bulldozers among the temple ruins. An archaeologist reminded us that a dig is a delicate but deliberate procedure. What might look like rubble to us is treasure to the archaeologist. An enormous amount of energy, time, and money is spent to dig, to uncover, to unearth antiquity—the forgotten, the beginnings of eras.

The stones of Solomon's temple were not hauled away when the Babylonians destroyed it in 586 B.C. Rather, the rubble was covered to make roads for the conquerors. Moreover, when Babylon was defeated by the Syrians, the Zerubbabel Temple of Nehemiah's day was constructed on the old site of Solomon's Temple.

Would you believe the news this morning says that twenty-five people were killed, and more than fifty were wounded, because the heirs of Abraham cannot reconcile their differences. As we search through the rubble of our minds, we search for answers to questions like, Why did this tragic bombing take place so near to the site of the yellow bulldozers?

We find the Gospel of John speaking to our query in chapter 4. The story takes Jesus through Samaria: "He had to go through Samaria" (4:4). Here in Samaria, Jesus figuratively bulldozes the "isms" that create the almost impenetrable layers that separate us from the God who made us, and from our kinfolk in the Spirit. We have lost the direction of the Creator's purpose for our being.

The first "ism" that Jesus addressed is the layer of overly ethnocentric and class-centered *culturalism*. After the Assyrian conquest, many foreigners were brought in to settle the land once inhabited by Jews. The intermarriage of these foreigners with the Jews who had not been deported to Assyria was the basis for conflict that has continued to this day. The hatred was so strong in Jesus' day that the Jews who traveled north did everything to avoid traveling through Samaria, even walking an extra thirty or so miles to go around the region.

This, however, was an "ism" that Jesus had no reason to observe. Hence he "had" to go through Samaria. The division of the people because of the differences in culture and religion had caused holy wars, hopeless alliances, and divided families. Jesus' act of common sense, as well as love, bulldozed away the residues and encrustations of centuries of this "ism."

Still, we are familiar with this kind of division. Right here in New York, I have seen debilitating conflict between tenement dwellers and brownstone owners. The blue collar and the white collar workers of Detroit, the street dwellers and the boulevard strollers of Los Angeles, and the farmers and the CEOs of Nebraska are all prone to the same kind of division. Not only has the Amtrak route delineated residences into preferred and not-preferred sides of the city, God's people have divided themselves by the culturalism of economic class. It is hard to escape the conclusion that Jesus' bulldozer has not been there yet but needs to come soon!

We return to the well. Next Jesus asked the Samaritan woman for a drink of water. No respectable Jewish man would talk to a lone woman, to say nothing of a Samaritan woman. It was also despicable for a Jewish man to ask a foreigner for a gift of hospitality of any kind, including a cool drink in the heat of the day. But Jesus did. And in so doing, his bulldozer pushed away accretions of sexism that date all the way back to the beginnings of the tradition that women are property. Jesus also pushed away colorism, the inside-the-race distinctions of complexion. Samaritan Jews, by mixing with the original Canaanites of Samaria, had acquired blacker skin tones. Jesus' ease of relating to this woman at the well indicates that his bulldozer pushed away colorism, too.

Jesus asks us to do likewise. We cannot be messengers of the faith while some people in our faith community are regarded by us as second class because of their gender. Theologian James Cone, in *For My People,* asks, "What is it that blinds black men to the truth regarding the suffering of their sisters?" But in addition to divisions based on gender, we make distinctions based on skin color. The fact that "paper bag" congregations still exist in the United States is deplorable. (The antebellum image of light-skinned house slaves and dark-skinned field slaves is the source of "paper bag" societies. All blacks darker than a paper bag were discouraged from seeking membership.)

Jesus still bulldozes the accumulations of color-conscious self-hatred in our African American societies and churches. He uncovers whatever hinders us from being of one accord in one place in worship. "The hour is coming when the true worshipers will worship the Father in spirit and truth" (4:23).

There is one more layer of spiritual rubble, the layer that is perhaps the most delicate but that most needs to be uncovered. In modern psychological terms, this rubble is called narcissism—

whatever moves us away from God, or thinking that the world revolves only around ourselves.

Jesus said to the Samaritan woman, "If you knew the gift of God, and who it is that is saying to you, 'Give me a drink,' you would have asked him, and he would have given you living water" (v. 10). But the woman, because of her self-centered, self-protecting defenses, was about to ruin a soul-saving encounter. I call it me-ism. This unnamed woman of Samaria did not speak as learnedly as the lawyer, Nicodemus, in John 3. But she was chatting with someone who did not relate according to status. This was someone who accepted and loved her in spite of who she was and what she had done, someone who could look beyond her faults and see her needs. There was no need for defensive me-ism. She could relax in the radiance of unconditional love.

When we see Jesus, who we are takes a back seat to who he is. The uncovering of my me-ism, my importance, allows me to understand the fact that it is okay if I am less wealthy than, less attractive than, less educated than. . . . Jesus is able to bulldoze below the coverings into my real business as a person. He is able to deal with the wounds and cuts and bruises. I am made whole by God's amazing grace!

I celebrate the repair of the city. I celebrate the repair of the culture—no more sexism, no more racism or colorism, no more me-ism. This morning I look across to the old city, and I see no temple! Jesus has bulldozed it all, and he prepares in me a temple. Through grace, my life is completely restored through our Lord and Savior, Jesus the Christ. My temple is a place where God dwells, a place where there is peace and love and joy! Hallelujah! Amen!

Question: In our highly technological era, in which we are capable of seemingly unlimited feats, are there limits to what we should do that are well inside the limits of what we could do? Are we in charge of the spark of life, or is the creator?

Remember Who Made Us

Teresa L. Fry

Pericope: Jeremiah 18:1-12

And the vessel that he made of clay was marred in the hand of the potter: so he made it again another vessel, as seemed good to the potter to make it (Jeremiah 18:4 NRSV).

R ead the newspaper. Watch television. Drive or walk down the street. Sit in a meeting. Go to church. Every place we turn it seems to happen. We can't avoid it. We can run but we can't hide from genetic engineering, test tube fertilization, assisted suicide, birth control, abortions, emotionless homicides, deserted elders, abusive adults, life-draining addictions, polluted environments. The list goes on. In our instantaneous, computerized, technology-based society, many of us seem to have come to believe that we created life and therefore are free to end it, modify it, destroy it, or mold it into anything we choose. My brothers and my sisters, the Lord has a flashing light at the end of our contemporary tunnel that cautions us, "Remember who made you!"

A familiar saying in Ecclesiastes has it that there is nothing new under the sun (1:9). Walk back with me now for a brief time through the sacred text, to the time of the weeping prophet, Jeremiah. It was some 2620 years ago, a time just like today: The people had spiritual amnesia. They had forgotten who made them, who brought them out of bondage, and whose they were. Jeremiah was serving as a prophet to Judah, the Southern Kingdom of Israel. Israel was ruled by an evil king, Jehoiakim. Jeremiah was troubled. He had complained to God about the people, and God had only told him that things would get worse before they got better. Only a few listened to Jeremiah's warnings that God was not pleased.

The *Jerusalem Daily News* reported on the great acts of men and sometimes women but failed to lift up any of the Word or the mighty acts of God. Those who went to worship rushed, because they did not want to take too much time. Priests were more concerned with the size of the offerings than with the care of the people. People forgot that Scripture said "In the beginning *God*" and took credit for how well the world was put together. The people were stiff-necked and hard-hearted and acted as if they had pulled themselves up by their own proverbial boot straps.

God sent a message to Jeremiah. Judah must repent, or it would be destroyed like a pot that is not up to the potter's standards. God created the world, and God can destroy it and use the broken clay to make a better world. So Jeremiah kept on preaching and doing what God said. God kindly sent a warning before the judgment came.

You've no doubt heard the story. One night Jeremiah had a dream that he was in the Hinnom Valley south of Jerusalem, near the pool of Siloam. God spoke to him in a parable: "Go down to the potter's house, and there I'll give you a message. Don't ask questions. Just go because I AM sent you." As Jeremiah reported it, "So I went."

Now, there were several pottery shops in the city, but Jeremiah was directed by the Holy Spirit down the potters' street to watch a particular potter at work. The process seemed simple enough: The potter selects clay, moist earth, or clean, water-borne clay, which is natural cut, rich clay found in the valley. Or he begins with prepared dory clay by sifting it and removing all foreign matter—rocks, twigs, anything that will prevent the clay from sticking together as it is left to stand in water to achieve uniform granules, or anything that will bump up on the wheel. The potter's mixture is left alone, set aside, to congeal, to achieve uniform texture, and to blend to the right consistency. The potter mixes the clay again, kneads it, and works out the air bubbles by treading on it or by working it in the palms of his hands. When the potter begins to create a vessel from the clay, sometimes the clay seems to have a mind of its own and isn't malleable. The potter moves it one way, and it winds up going the opposite direction—just like some of us. Finally, the vessel is finished and set aside to dry.

Strangely enough, the potter doesn't always detect defects until the drying process. Sometimes, even years later in the aging process faults begin to show up. The clay is marred. The potter can either permit the defects to stay, or reshape the vessel by watering it down or breaking it and starting all over again.

Another drying method can then be used to decrease the water in the clay mixture. The vessel, jar, or pot will then be fired in a closed or open oven or kiln. This process hardens the vessel and helps it hold its shape, to attain a leather-like finish, and to stand up under constant use. Sometimes the potter will cover the dried vessel with a glaze to seal all the cracks both inside and out.

Everything the potter will create will have a use. Even broken, old pottery is fixed with wires to hold it together. If it's too old or has too many pieces, those pieces are used as jar covers, instruments to cook, clean, write, or dispense medicine.

My sisters and my brothers, we are the clay, dirt and water mixed together in the hands of the almighty Potter. We must remember that we did not create ourselves. Whoever or whatever we are today, it is because of the Master Potter who made each of us, unique and marvelously well. Each of us has a function regardless of our age, race, gender, size, shape, or color. No one else can decide our usefulness; only the potter who made us can decide.

Where did you get that idea, preacher? Well, the book of
Genesis records that having created the world and all within it, on
the afternoon of the sixth day God said, "Let us make humankind
in our image, according to our likeness. . . . So God created
humankind in God's image, . . . male and female he created them"
(Genesis 1:26-27 NRSV). God created man (*ish*) and woman
(*ishshah*) from the same ingredients, dirt (*adamah*).

In Genesis 2 we read that God scooped the dirt from the banks
of the rivers that flowed out of the Garden of Eden. God carefully
sifted it back and forth, back and forth, to rid it of anything that
would contaminate it. God worked to sift out traits like greed,
selfishness, jealousy, hatred, and envy. Then God took the water
of the spirit and mixed it with the dirt, and continued to work it
in the divine hands. God made man and woman, differing only in
their reproductive organs. One flesh they were, so that we would
be interdependent—woman brought out of man, and man brought
out of woman. No man, no woman; no woman, no man. It's a
mutuality thing. It's about equality and kinship.

I envision God working over the clay, putting on the parts as
God determined: 206 bones, 880 muscles, 320 nerves, 294 arter-
ies, 87 veins, one heart, one brain, two lungs, and two kidneys,
covered with four layers of skin, and topped off with protective
hair. The divine Potter then gives each vessel distinctive features.
Some have broad bases, small tops, short handles, medium thickness; some are round, square, long, short—each in the image and
likeness of God. Then God sets the vessels aside to begin to dry,
to firm up their form for a period, in preparation for the world,
usually for nine months. Each vessel has an opening in the top to
hold oil, water, or even air (symbols of the Holy Spirit). Each has
handles or projections to reach toward something, perhaps to hold
on to God's unchanging hand. Then God paints each inside and
outside with the Spirit, so that no weapon formed against the
vessels shall prosper. Others may seek to smash God's vessels,
but the treasure within lives on.

The vessel is not finished until the Potter says so, just as babies
are not born until God says so. No amount of technology can give

or take life fully until the Creator moves. When the vessel is done, when the fullness of time has come, God the Potter places a seal on the top of each vessel—"Handmade by God"—so that everyone knows who and whose we are.

Just before God fires us in the kiln of the Holy Spirit, God burnishes us, places a glaze over us to hold moisture, and then the final firing protects us from the knocks and disappointments of life. The Potter distinguishes the vessels by the glaze on the outside. Some are ivory, alabaster, cinnamon, cherry, oak, chocolate, mahogany, onyx, all beautiful, all valued beings in God's creation.

Way back in the Garden of Eden, God named the two created beings Adam ("man" or "human") and Eve ("woman" or "life"), setting the creative pattern. God called them by name, just as we are known by our names. Genesis says that God was pleased with creation and gave them the position of caretakers *(rada)* over all God's earthly kingdom (vv. 29-31). These were not positions of domination but of dominion and responsibility.

My brothers and my sisters, we are to care for God's earth just as we are to care for each other. God made each of us a little lower than the angels, and has crowned us with glory and honor (Psalm 8:5). We share power over creation, but we are not God, no matter what we tell ourselves. We may tamper with God's creation plan, but do not have the authority to change it. We keep trying to improve on what God has already done. The message is the same as in the day of Jeremiah. Remember who made us.

God places us where God wants us, ordering our steps in God's service. We are called to teach, preach, serve, heal, prophesy, sing, listen, dance, or even wave a handkerchief witnessing the goodness of God as God sees fit. God makes, calls, anoints, appoints, ordains, directs, equips, and protects each vessel—man and woman—according to God's will and plan for our lives. No need to argue. No need for discussions. No need for defensiveness. We work best in the role for which we were made.

Like Jeremiah when God gave him instruction, we, too, must say, "So I went. . . ." Whatever God tells us to do is what we are to do, even in this technical age. It was God who created the entire miracle of technology. Wherever God tells us to go is where we are to go. Whenever God says work, we must be ready to work. God never overlooks a vessel, because God knows the needs and uses for each. When confusion is all around, problems lie on every hand, night is too long, burdens are too heavy, the body is breaking down, we need to stop and ponder and realize who made us. Who fashioned us? Who framed us? Who molded us? Who shaped and reshaped us? We must remember who and whose we are.

Likewise, because we are treasured works of the divine hand, no one can abuse us, disrespect us (verbally or physically), manipulate us, expel us, or do anything else detrimental in the name of love or any other principle, and yet claim to be in God's will. We are the precious children of God. We do not own each other. We are called to appreciate, to love God's unique gifts of life, to see God in each of our brothers and sisters.

We are earthen vessels, dirt, dust, and far from perfect. Every now and then we need to visit the Potter's house—God's rehabilitation unit. In our aging process we may develop cracks in our vessels, leaks in our lids, and fractures in our handles. Even those of us who have been saved, sanctified, and filled with the Holy Ghost need a checkup at the Potter's house. We will then remember who made us. God's love, power, grace, spirit, and healing touch can restore us to usefulness. Only our Creator/Potter can repair. Only God can redeem, reconstruct, renew, and regenerate.

We are not the first nor will we be the last to be shaped and molded by the Potter. The foremothers and forefathers knew about the Master's touch. When they were told they were nobody, nothing, less than human, they remembered who made them and stood boldly as children of the Most High God. I can hear them calling across the ages to their sophisticated, educated, often privileged grandchildren and great grandchildren, reminding us that God made us and we did not make ourselves. And as the psalmist said, "We are fearfully and wonderfully made" (139:14 NRSV).

When it seemed like the world would drown in a sea of transgression and oppression, as in Jeremiah's time, the Potter had a plan to remold humanity as he saw fit. God placed a creative spark in the womb of a young virgin named Mary. As that infant grew, the world began to be reshaped. As the Potter's assistant, Jesus, even the Christ, made it possible for each of us to have eternal life—men and women, black and white, rich and poor, educated and uneducated, able and disabled—as part of God's, not humanity's, plan.

He came so that when this vessel is destroyed, is no longer of any earthly use, has been broken, battered and worn—when this old earthly vessel is discarded—we have another vessel or building, not made by human hands, which is eternal in heaven. And we shall praise the Potter there, forever and ever. Hallelujah! Amen!

Question: Is there anything one could have or achieve that is more important than the task God has assigned each of us? Is it anachronistic piety, absolutely obsolete for our times, to view the claims of God for our lives as high favor, and to place those claims ahead of all else?

Favor with God

Janette Hightower

Pericope: Luke 1:26-38

And the angel came to her and said, Hail, thou that art highly favored, the Lord is with thee: blessed art thou among women (Luke 1:28).

Favor with God implies blessed events—out of the ordinary, uncommon, extraordinary, unusual, notable events. Certainly when most of us were preparing for our marriage to Mr. or Mrs. Wonderful, we felt we had found favor with God, maybe even a double portion of God's favor. We thought, "As wonderful as he or she is, God has certainly smiled on me to give me this person for a husband or wife." We were excited, we felt blessed, we embraced the future. We had found favor with God.

Marriage begins with a vow, a commitment to love, honor, and cherish. While this is a part of what some of us expect from marriage today, that is not how marriage began in biblical times. Mary, according to Scripture, was "espoused" to Joseph. She was handpicked or designated for Joseph. I do not get the impression that Mary sat around in her bedroom writing her name as it would appear: Mrs. Joseph of Nazareth. I am unable to find scriptural support for any excitement at all from Mary regarding this marriage. It appears to have been a marriage of arrangement, which was not at all uncommon for those times. Perhaps Mary's father and her intended husband, Joseph, had met in the green pastures of Nazareth and had made a gentlemen's agreement. The price for Mary had been negotiated fairly between the two men, her father and her husband-to-be. Joseph had paid the dowry, which was what that transaction was called, and the status of the relationship between Mary and Joseph was that Mary was espoused or promised in marriage to Joseph. That meant more than engaged but not yet married. This espousal was an arrangement in which she could not participate. She could not reject; she could not abandon. She had no other option.

We don't really know, but we like to imagine that Mary had no qualms about the matter. Joseph was a good provider. He was the town's carpenter. We also imagine that Mary probably didn't have the passion of David and Bathsheba or Samson and Delilah, nor would she have had the anticipation for Joseph that she might have had for a person of her own choice. There were no hearts drawn with Mary and Joseph's names inside, no scented pillows with their names craftily embroidered, no tree trunks roughly etched with "Mary loves Joseph." Nobody claimed to have seen the palms of Joseph's hands where he had written in ink: "Joseph 'n' Mary." There were none of our day's visible signs that these two belonged together.

Clearly, though, Mary was willing to honor the contract her father and Joseph had negotiated. Women in those days needed a male to validate their existence. The male was needed for provision, protection, and procreation. The male's supplying of these needs did not require her to love the male. This was highly respected tradition, and it was accepted as such. Without a father or a husband to provide for and protect her, Mary could have been forced to fend for herself. She could have been forced to become a public prostitute or met some other undesirable fate. With this marriage contract, Mary was contented, satisfied, safe, and to some degree at least, excited. This was her first and only marriage.

Then one day, as she sat alone in her father's house in Nazareth, the angel Gabriel spoke to Mary: "Hail, thou that art highly favored, the Lord is with thee: blessed art thou among women." Mary's response to the angel was the same as yours or mine would be: she was awestricken. Gabriel calmly assured her: "Fear not, Mary: for thou hast found favor with God. Behold thou shalt conceive in thy womb, and bring forth a son, and shalt call his name Jesus." The angel elaborated further, and Mary's jaw dropped as far as it could drop.

Mary got her nerve up and asked, "How in the world could all of this be, considering the fact that I haven't even had relations with a man yet?" Gabriel responded: "The Holy Ghost shall come upon thee, and the power of the Highest shall overshadow thee: therefore also that holy thing which shall be born of thee shall be called the Son of God." Gabriel told Mary also about her cousin Elizabeth, who though previously barren and in old age, was already six months pregnant. Elizabeth's miracle being established made Mary's more credible, and Mary finally accepted and acknowledged her favor with God, albeit with less than great enthusiasm. She said, "Be it unto me according to thy word." Mary did not sound quite as reluctant as if she had said, in the words of our hood, "You the one that's doing the talking."

The angel departed and so did Mary. She went into the hill country into a city of Judah, and she entered the house of Zacharias and Elizabeth. As Mary greeted her pregnant cousin, Elizabeth, the babe leaped for joy in Elizabeth's womb. It was like a kick in the stomach, and without intending to speak so loudly, cousin Elizabeth almost yelled the same words that the angel Gabriel had spoken to Mary at Nazareth: "Blessed art thou among women, and blessed is the fruit of thy womb."

This, too, was awesome. Elizabeth had not had any encounter with the angel. She knew nothing about what had happened to Mary, except for what her unborn baby had implied with his kick. Furthermore, at that time, Mary did not know that she herself was pregnant. It was overwhelming enough for Mary to be unmarried and pregnant. But that's not all. She was unmarried, pregnant, and the baby's father was not the man to whom she was engaged. Plus the baby's father was not even a man! Who would believe her? I can hear the street committee and the grapevine people with their interpretations of that story: "Joseph's fiancee has been a little indiscreet." Of course, we don't want to quote them exactly.

Now the Bible tells us that Mary stayed with Elizabeth for three months. Again, we can easily imagine why Mary would have done that. Mary needed Elizabeth to help her know what to expect during her pregnancy, and how to deal with her soon-to-become husband. She needed Elizabeth to explain with words and with deeds what it means to feel your body invaded by another body. Mary needed Elizabeth the same way our youth today need the wealth of wisdom and the wit of our senior citizens.

But most of all Mary needed her senior cousin to help her know how to handle this blessing of favor with God. "Mary, you do carry the very Word of God in your womb. Mary, never let anyone prevent you from preaching or teaching or showing or telling the world about the baby whom you carried in your womb. Mary, you do not need permission to do what God has commissioned you to do. You shall call His name Jesus, the Savior of his people."

What do we have to say to Mary, the mother of our Lord, at this important time in her life? Maybe this. "Mary, listen to Elizabeth. You cannot do everything everyone else does and then find favor with God. Mary, you are blessed among women. You are set aside for sacred use. That doesn't mean you will never have fun. It means the things it takes for others supposedly to enjoy themselves are not the things God has designed for your very interesting and abundant life. Your favor with God includes a different dimension. Mary, you and Elizabeth have both been filled with the Holy Spirit."

As Elizabeth's time drew near for the delivery of her baby, Mary was there to help her. Elizabeth's spiritual wisdom continued to flow, and Mary continued to listen to her intently. Mary became more and more convinced that she had indeed found favor with God. While her future life was to be nothing like what little she had dared to dream for herself before, she knew now that the favor of God and the calling of God exceeded all she had ever dared to ask or think. Her almost reluctant consent to Gabriel, "Be it unto me according to thy word," now became a powerful affirmation.

Mary remembered that first day when Cousin Liz had helped her to know how great it was to be favored and called of God, and that it was the Holy Spirit at work in her. She sang that same hymn over and over again: "My soul doth magnify the Lord, and my spirit hath rejoiced in God my Savior."

Quilting the Life of a Virtuous Woman

Marjorie B. Lewis

Pericopes: Proverbs 31: 10-11; Philippians 4:11-13

Who can find a virtuous woman? (Proverbs 31:10).

Giving reverence to God our Creator, Parent, and Salvation, I am thankful for the honor of preaching this eulogy for my mama, Helena Munn Dunham Lewis. Responding to those who are surprised that I have found the courage to do this, let me humbly say that I find it easy. I consider her one of the greatest people I have ever known, and I hold a strong Christian belief in eternal life. I accept her passing as a blessing—part of the overall blessing of God's gift of life. I believe that my mama has been healed and freed from her physical suffering, and so this is an occasion to celebrate her life on this earth with these words of eulogy.

This does not mean, of course, that I will not or have not shed tears, but I do take serious hope in her transformation from this life on earth to her eternal life. So at this parting, won't you join me while we quilt, as it were, Scripture passages to which her life gives witness and fresh meaning?

The apostle Paul declares to the church at Philippi that his communication is not because he is in want:

> For I have learned, in whatsoever state I am, therewith to be content. I know both how to be abased, and I know how to abound: everywhere and in all things I am instructed both to be full and to be hungry, both to abound and to suffer need. I can do all things [I can take or cope with any condition] through Christ which strengtheneth me. (Philippians 4:11-13)

Mama had the opposite of the haughtiness that the Word declares will bring God's displeasure. Throughout books like the Proverbs, such behavior is associated with insecurity, ashamedness, or discontent with an unfulfilled life. Helena was quite the other way, never seeming either unfulfilled or ashamed. She coped graciously with conditions all the way from humble beginnings to a position as one of the most powerful black women in this country. And she climaxed it all with her victorious testimony of dignity and contentment in a wheel chair. She was a modern embodiment of these words, "I can do all things—I can take or cope with any condition—through Christ who strengthens me."

Before this statement, Paul had said he knew how to be humble. In modern, everyday language, he knew how to be subtle instead of bodaciously self-assertive, how to make people comfortable in his presence. He unashamedly combined a high social standing and excellent education with manual labor, working on tents.

Mama had this subtlety, too. Part of it was manifest in the fact that she could relate to anyone—rich or poor, old or young, religious or profane, strong or weak, black or white, male or female. She showed all of them a way to relate to her and be comfortable. She simply and humbly subdued the part of her that was in contrast to them, and she opened up the aspects of her person and life that were in common with whoever it was. Humility like this is a very powerful human trait.

One day I asked my daddy, "Why did you marry Mama?" His response was quite to the point: "We had a lot in common, and I felt comfortable around her." I have often reflected on that comment. And I'm quite sure almost every member of this congregation could say the same thing. Like Paul, she knew the subtleties of healthy humility, how to be humble without losing dignity or effectiveness as a person, increasing both dignity and effectiveness, in fact. Paul also said, no doubt humbly, that he knew how to abound—how to be in possession of much and in high station. We know little of his high station in life before the Damascus Road, but we do know that he worked with his own hands to support not only himself but his entire company while he was in Corinth.

Mama was like that. She never waited to be asked to help others. Like the woman in Proverbs 31:20, she stretched forth her hand to the poor and needy, in addition to being generous with her family. For those of other stations in life but in need of professional help and advice, she was only too happy to assist without consulting fee. She helped with taxes as well as sewing, with editorial work as well as cooking, with counseling as well as cleaning. She had so many ways to help, and she found joy not in accumulating things but in seeing her family and community fulfilled.

It could be that her most important assistance was to the downhearted, those in spiritual need. She and Daddy developed our home into a one-stop encouragement-as-well-as-assistance center. They were ready and able to help almost anybody with almost any kind of need.

As I reflect on how Mama knew how to handle abundance, I am reminded of the Land of Sausa, in African tradition. It's the place where *some* people go after death. But it's not for everybody; there are conditions. The tradition says that many of the good works we admire—high moral and ethical standards, honesty, even faithful attendance at church—won't get a person into the Land of Sausa. There has to be some *person* left on earth who has a part of the departed still living in her or him. It's not greatly different from the Last Judgment in Matthew 25:34-36, where people like Mama were told:

> Come, ye blessed of my Father, inherit the kingdom
> prepared for you from the foundation of the world: for I

was hungry, and ye gave me meat: I was thirsty, and ye
gave me drink: . . . naked, and ye clothed me. . .

One other reflection on Mama compels our attention. It has to
do with the implications of our scriptural text, but it involves also
what may be a completely fresh comparison of the strengths and
meanings of roles assigned to women in traditional and contemporary thought. We have already looked together at the ability to
do all things, to take any stress, to cope with whatever—in the
strength of Christ. But we need to return to this passage and focus
its light on the widespread controversy concerning the image and
role of the ideal woman in our society.

You see, Mama might have been mistaken for the old traditional ideal wife and mother: easy-going, naive, self-effacing, and
subject to exploitation. But I would submit that her ability to be
low-key and subtle was a more effective model by far than the
blatant, angry woman or man who tries instantaneously to change
the world for the better. Those who mistook her subtle approach
for weakness have much to learn.

Subtlety is a trait and tool of the powerful. Mama's subtlety
was a quiet indication of her own awareness of the power of God
at work within her. Jesus, often seen in this same mode, offered
his similar advice in these words: "Be ye therefore wise as
serpents, and harmless as doves" (Matthew 10:16). The wisdom
and power of God advise and allow us to be subtle in our dealings
with God's people. What better way to demonstrate our faith in
the power and providence of God? This was Mama's unforgetta-
ble gift, but it was not what I would dare call unique. Untold
thousands of black women have demonstrated similar gifts.

Many wonder where the strength of black women has come
from. Years of abuse and oppression did not destroy your spirits.
You became lovably strong women with the strength to love
others. You are an inspiration to those who face the same obstacles, so they can continue on anyhow. The pain has made many
of you an inspiration that will live on in others for generations yet
to come.

One has to wonder where your strength came from, Helena, when the dominant culture was poised in subtle ways to destroy your very personhood. They tried to teach you self-hate. But Mama, you held your head high, and whenever we see a proud black girl or woman, we will remember you and the dignity and self-confidence you inspired.

Mama, how did you and so many like you turn out to be giants in professional fields ordinarily reserved for males or whites only? Refusing to yield to the expectations of others, you have courageously and quietly plugged on, in the raw belief that the very power of God would help in a just cause. When it was clearly necessary, you have stood up and fought in the open for what you knew to be righteous and just. You have embraced the risk and taken up the cross, walking on through the wind and rain to achieve the dream. Whenever we see the strength of African American sisters swimming upstream daily in our still repressive society, we'll see you and be blessed by your memory.

Then finally, Mama, many no doubt have wondered what made you strong enough to accomplish so much and yet be a loving wife and mother. You carried all of this responsibility without anger or bitterness or insensitivity. You have blessed my daddy with forty-six years of peace and joy, and together you have raised four children, giving them and many others both strength and high principles.

You have moved on to heaven, but we'll see you in youth who have respect for elders, and who also have the drive and determination to break through barriers and achieve. Mama, your life will be with us as long as we live, and may your model of liberated living abound among us all, female and male as well. We pray that your peaceful ways and power to cause change will inspire all of us to use the same tactics and follow the same Christ whom you served so well.

Enjoy heaven; enjoy Sausa; and watch for us. We plan to meet you there.

Question: What is the position of people with AIDS in the sight of God? If the Spirit says "Whosoever will, let him take the water of life freely" (Revelation 22:17), and if Magic Johnson can be fully accepted in the National Basketball Association, is not the church likewise obligated to proclaim God's love for the person with AIDS, regardless of the circumstances of infection?

Witness for the Defense

Kathi E. Martin

Pericope: Romans 8:31-39

For I am convinced that neither death, nor life, nor angels, nor rulers, nor things present, nor things to come, nor powers, nor height, nor depth, nor anything else in all creation, will be able to separate us from the love of God in Christ Jesus our Lord (Romans 8:38-39 NRSV).

My name is Vincent. Lately I have had occasion to watch television more frequently than in the past. One thing that's new to me is the presence of cameras in the courtroom. Every now and then, the news broadcasts include footage of actual trials. Whether the accused is being tried for murder or something else, the trials have one thing in common: somebody found himself or herself in a situation full of trouble. Guilty or not guilty, the person on trial is beset with mental and even physical pain and embarrassment. The accused sits there at the mercy of the court, waiting to see whether he or she will be released or convicted. In some cases the decision is a matter of life or death. Although we hope people are not put on trial for crimes they did not commit, we know that does happen. And although we hope that justice then works and the innocent are ultimately found not guilty, we know that sometimes the innocent are punished—and even put to death.

As a matter of fact, all of us at times find ourselves in trouble and pain—sometimes physical pain, sometimes emotional pain. Often we find ourselves in a state of trouble that we do not understand at all. We don't understand it; we don't deserve it; we don't know why it is here; and we don't know what the outcome will be. We feel just like we are sitting in a court room, helpless and falsely accused.

I frequently have days like that. You see, I am a thirty-two-year-old African American man living with AIDS. Many days my body is physically drained. That does not, however, compare to the emotional pain inflicted by former loved ones who avoid me or continually blame me for my illness. Even my church refuses to embrace me. So often I am left alone with my pain and my fears, feeling sentenced to a life of isolation. After so much rejection, I even begin to wonder whether God cares about me and my situation.

During those times, I wish I could go to some sort of life court to prove my innocence. Perhaps then I could get release from these painful situations and accusations. In Paul's letter to the church at Rome, he uses the image of just such a court situation.

Imagine that we are in a court room. The judge is in place. The jury has been selected. I am sitting in the chair next to my defense attorney, waiting for the prosecutor to present the case against me. I do not even understand what the charges are; I just know the effects are pain, rejection, and isolation.

The prosecutor makes an opening statement. "Ladies and gentlemen of the jury, today we are going to prove that the difficulty in Vincent's life is his own willful waywardness, and that he is no longer worthy of God's love."

Then my defense attorney makes an opening statement. She

looks first at the judge, then the jury, and says, "What are we to say to these things? If God is for us, who is against us?" (Romans 8:31 NRSV).

The prosecution lays out the case against me, trying to show that I must have done something to bring about the level of pain, isolation, and rejection I am experiencing. The prosecutor is even trying to prove that the God and Parent of us all must be against me. He is going so far as to try to convince me, the defendant, that I am guilty and without hope.

The prosecution lines up various witnesses against me. The first witness is my friend, who does not understand why I do not go out or take her places like I used to do. "He used to be available for me every time I called. He used to lend me money when I needed it. He used to listen to all of my problems. Lately he has just been different and distant." She does not understand that my illness often leaves me too tired to do all of the activities that I used to do. I cannot even work consistently to care for myself financially.

The second witness is my sister, with whom I often have conflicts. "Vincent is a very angry young man. Sometimes we argue for hours. He is just so stubborn and mean these days. He can only see things his way." She is careful not to testify that she starts those arguments. Basically, the anger is hers, because it hurts her to think her brother is sick. She cannot accept the reality of my illness.

The third witness is my old Sunday school teacher. He states, "Vincent was always a good student growing up. He was very active in the church. He was a junior usher, a junior trustee, and he was always in Sunday School. He studied the lessons well and was always a Christian young man. As he got older, he must have turned away from God. He started living his life in ways that are contrary to what he learned as a child. That is why he is infected. He strayed away from God."

That witness really starts to break me down. The church has always been my place of refuge in times of trouble. Although I have not literally and intentionally turned clear away from God by my life choices, perhaps there was some truth to what my old teacher is saying. I have started to doubt that I am really worthy of God's love.

Then the prosecutor calls me to the stand. His intent is to try to convince me of my own guilt, to make me truly believe that I am unworthy of God's love. He suggests, "Look at your life; you have had 'hardship, distress, persecution, famine, nakedness, peril, and sword.' You have no money. You can barely afford to support yourself. You suffer from periods of loneliness and depression. You have lost many of your friends. Your family does not understand you. Many are afraid even to be around you. You have been the victim of violence due to your illness and your life choices. Surely you cannot still believe God loves you! Why would God permit these sufferings if God loves you? Surely you have heard that bad things happen to us because we deserve them."

The prosecutor's line of reasoning is a legal stunt that he often uses to try to break people like me down. He tries to make us give up and become suicidal by making us feel guilty and beyond God's love. And sometimes we actually begin to believe that God's love is really no longer available to us.

But just then, when I have begun to doubt myself and my worth in God's eyes, my attorney starts her defense:

"'What then are we to say to these things? If God is for us, who is against us? He who did not withhold his own Son, but gave him up for all of us, will he not with him also give us everything else? Who will bring any charge against God's elect? It is God who justifies. Who is to condemn?' (vv. 31-33 NRSV).

"Ladies and gentlemen of the jury, it is my intent to prove that Vincent is still loved by God. To defend this case I need only to call one witness to the stand. I only need to call Jesus to the stand as a character witness for the defense because we know, 'it is Christ Jesus who died, yes, who was raised, who is at the right hand of God, who indeed intercedes for us'" (v. 34 NRSV).

How wonderful it is to see Jesus take the stand in my defense. After all the hurt and rejection, to see Jesus stand in defense of me is awesome encouragement. Suddenly it doesn't matter that others have turned away. The pain actually seems more bearable, because I do not feel like I am alone any more. And the One who is with me is no less than the very Son of God.

Then Jesus begins to speak, "I know Vincent. I remember when he made his decision to walk with me. I have heard the many times he has prayed for healing and comfort. I have heard his cries of loneliness. I have even heard his prayers for those who have rejected him. Surely he has made some unwise choices, to say the very least, as all humans do, but that does not mean he is to be denied God's love."

Then Jesus continues, "But with all I know about Vincent, I love him. As a child of God, he is my brother. Vincent is made worthy of God's love and grace, because I went through suffering and persecution for him. I endured betrayal for him. I was convicted for him. I hung on a cross and died for him. I know Vincent very well, and regardless of what others may say, I know him as a child of God."

Then the defense makes a closing statement: "'For your sake we are being killed all day long; we are accounted as sheep to be slaughtered' (v. 36 NRSV).

"We are all human. We know life is going to have its moments of pain and trouble. We do not look at all these things as punishment from God, or even as reaping what we sow. When what we see as undeserved trouble comes, we do not waste our energies trying to figure why it happened, or asking, 'How did God do this to me?' Those types of thoughts drain us, cause us to be nonproductive, and foster feelings of uselessness and hopelessness. This is not to say we should gladly accept persecution. This is not to say we enjoy pain and trouble. We do not. But if we concentrate on pain and focus on trouble, we will not realize the sources of comfort and strength that are available to us. We will not feel the love and support that God is trying to provide."

Well, the prosecution has presented the case against me. He has tried to prove that under no circumstances should I receive God's love. He has stated that if I do not live my life according to other people's expectations, then I must be unforgivably guilty. He has tried to point out that the distress in my life is a result of God's wrathful punishment, not just the result of an unwise choice. The prosecution would be most dismayed if he were to apply his own rules to all of his own mistakes, to say nothing of his own grievous sins.

Then the defense has presented a case to prove God's love for me. Even Jesus took the stand to intercede for me and prove my standing as a child of God. But, my brothers and sisters, that is not all. I can now face my accusers without fearing their rejection or persecution. I can bear my illness and the uncertainty of the future. Regardless of what the verdict is, regardless of what others' opinions may be, I know for myself that God loves me.

Yes, trouble may come, and yes, there are going to be painful times. No, I do not like it, and I might not think I deserve it, but I can face the trials that come my way as long as I love and trust God, and know that God loves me. I can look to the future and say with that famous survivor of trouble, the apostle Paul:

> In all these things we are more than conquerors through Him who loved us. For I am convinced that neither death, nor life, nor angels, nor rulers, nor things present, nor things to come, nor powers, nor height, nor depth, nor anything else in creation, will be able to separate us from the love of God in Christ Jesus our Lord. (vv. 37-39 NRSV)

Question: Is there such a person as a transgressor too far outside our moral code to be sought and served and restored?

Human Reclamation

Ella Pearson Mitchell

Pericope: Luke 7:36-50

And he said unto her, Thy sins are forgiven (Luke 7:48).

This morning I invite you to consider these words of Scripture from Luke 7:48, "And he said unto her, Thy sins are forgiven." Our theme is "God's Call to Reclamation and Restoration." In keeping with the thought of reclamation and restoration, let me share with you the complaint of a man who is desperately in need of restoration, now that he has been reclaimed. I read his appeal on behalf of the African American prison population in a great Christian magazine called *The Other Side*. He wrote of the painful plight of African Americans in jail—in the big house. Some of what he said is already well known.

You know the statistics. The United States is rapidly becoming the world's largest prison camp. Tragically, there are now more black men in prison than in the halls of higher education. The writer was one of these prisoners and is now a trained professional. He has already served twenty-two years in Sing Sing for murder, and he is still there. But he is at this writing a true believer. He has completed both college and seminary work while behind bars. In his recent article, he writes that after a riot over extremely poor living conditions in the prison, *none* of the inmates' letters to pastors and theologians were ever answered. No ministry was extended, except through his seminary, which already had a program within the prison's walls. In a word, the brothers and sisters in the big house are not taken seriously by the vast majority of African American churches.

We need to be seriously concerned for the large number of blacks who need to be reclaimed and who, we hope, will one day be released. And then think of all the others, male and female, who never go to jail but are lost—lost, I tell you, in the vicious culture of the ghetto street. We desperately need an entirely new agenda that focuses on reclaiming the sons and daughters of our Creator, no matter how they smell, what they look like, what their habits may be, or where they live. We, as a black church, with our inescapable involvement in our neighborhoods and communities, shall never be whole without those whom Jesus Christ calls us to reclaim. Our Lord himself was deep into the reclamation of souls.

Listen, if you will to the testimony of a woman who was once trapped in the street. They called her a sinner, a streetwalker, a woman of the night, a prostitute. I want to remind you of what Jesus did for her.

Although Brother Luke identifies me only as a nameless sinner, you may call me Hithpael, or "one who was sick with grief." I had earned a living in the street since I was fifteen. I had no choice; there were no secretary or clerk jobs. And there weren't any jobs open for baby-sitters or laundry women. But I had to have something to keep the family going. You see, Papa was dead, and I was the oldest child. My family depended on me just to keep them alive. Poor Mama had to take care of the younger children. There were no neighborhood child-care centers. And what's more, we wouldn't have had any money to pay for any kind of care.

At first, it wasn't so bad, something of an adventure. But it got to where every man who saw me seemed to sense who I was. They would almost automatically undress me with their lustful eyes, treating me like meat on a butcher's board. Oh, how I hated it! It got to where I simply couldn't stand it. If it hadn't been for my family, I might have taken my own life.

Then one day I met up with a man who was different—hear me, *very* different. His penetrating eyes looked not at my body but at my soul. He seemed to know all about me, yet he appeared to understand me, and he accepted me just as I was. It's like you say in your song: "He looked beyond my faults and saw my need." I had never felt so wonderful in all the days I had lived. I didn't want the feeling to end, not ever. I did everything I could to stay close to this man they called Jesus while he was still in our community. I needed to be near whenever he was preaching. I followed him! Yes, I stayed in his very tracks as much as I could, even when the street committee scoffed or scorned me. I felt like I was somebody! Yes, I was somebody!

It wasn't long before I heard that this teacher was invited to dinner in the house of a big-shot Pharisee named Simon. I wasn't invited, of course, because women were left out at most functions, especially women like me. But I walked on in anyhow. I was so glad to see Jesus that I just cried for joy. I know it looked strange, but I just kneeled there at his feet, crying. And the tears, they kept on a-coming, while he lay with his head toward the table.

Suddenly I noticed that my tears had splattered all over his dirty dusty feet, and when tears mixed with the sand, it made quite a mess. Oh, I felt so embarrassed; I had to do something quick. So I just wiped his feet with my hair. I was getting more and more embarrassed. Truth of the matter was that old Simon hadn't even attempted to wash Jesus' feet like he should have, after all that walking along the dusty road.

Then, as I held Jesus' feet, I caught myself kissing them. Imagine that! The guests just stared at me, but I couldn't help myself. And I'm so glad that Jesus didn't draw back or even push me away. He didn't seem to have any problem with what I was doing or what the stuck-up guests thought.

It was then that I really broke loose. I always carried this box of perfume with me, you know, in case I should need it. And all of a sudden, I didn't want to use that perfume on myself any more, ever. I just poured it out as ointment on Jesus' feet. I didn't care how much it had cost or how much I could have made with it. I was freed of all the pressures, I was reclaimed, and I didn't want any more of that old money or even the looks of those nasty old men.

When Simon saw me so close to his honored guest and realized who I was, that was just more than he could take. His face got all flushed, and he looked like he was going to explode any minute. Jesus read his mind and knew instantly just exactly what old Simon was thinking. That old geezer Simon was thinking that no real prophet would ever let such a woman get that close to him. But before he could say it, Jesus spoke up and answered his very thoughts. It was awesome!

Quietly and calmly, Jesus spoke to him: "Simon, I have something to tell you." Old Simon said, "Say on, teacher." Then Jesus began to tell him a story about a man who had loaned money to two people—one who owed five hundred pence and the other who owed fifty. Because neither one could pay him back, he kindly forgave both of them. He let them just keep the money. Jesus asked Simon which debtor would love the lender the more?

Old righteous Simon didn't know a good way to get out of that one, so he said, "I suppose the one who owed him the most." Jesus told him that was correct, and that ended the story but not the discussion. Jesus pushed on, to confront Simon about me: "Look, see this woman kneeling here? When I came into your house, you forgot to offer me the common courtesy of a vessel of water to wash my dusty feet. But she has washed them with her tears and wiped them with her hair. And I did not forget that you didn't even offer me the usual kiss of welcome. But she has kissed my feet again and again." I thought my Lord was finished, but he kept right on after Simon. "You didn't give me any oil for my head, but this woman has poured rare perfume on my *feet*."

Can you imagine how I felt? It was like a calm came over my troubled spirit—something I had never felt before. No one had ever been this kind or caring to me in all of my life. I had never been so received, so accepted, and so complimented by *anybody* in all of my twenty-five years! Think about it!

And then, would you believe, Jesus turned around and said, "Daughter, your sins are all forgiven." Now that's when this whole scene caused quite an uproar, 'cause those churchy folks didn't figure Jesus had any authority to be about forgiving anybody's sins. But that wasn't all Jesus said. He put his hand on my head and told me point blank, "My child, your faith has saved you this very day; go your way in peace."

You can't imagine what that meant to me. Here I was—one day considered human trash, and the next day reclaimed. I could go anywhere after that with my head up high. 'Cause one day I was a tramp, and the next I was a woman reclaimed and restored by no less a person than Jesus of Nazareth himself. One day I was little more than the meat on a butcher's board, and the next I was a woman of dignity and worth. I had a whole new idea of who I was and what I could do. I was reclaimed from the degradation of the streets and the awful inhumanity of being used by strange and violent men. I was made whole! Praise God!

And how did the family fare after that? Well, I am happy to report that there were now enough grown sons that I wasn't even tempted to go back to the streets to work. I had poured out all of my perfume, and I was saved. Praise God, I started living for Jesus ever since that night in Simon's house.

I don't know what the climate is like in your day where you are, but from my vantage point over here in the Glory Land, I know that, here and there, you have churches that are not like old Simon's church. I know of a church north of where you are, where drug dealers, ex-junkies, and drug addicts are welcome no matter how they smell or look. They can get a bath and a meal, and they also get love.

That seems to be the only strategy those church people have— reclaiming love. The pastor taught himself to keep calm and collected when the odors were almost unbearable. He knows they are somebody's son or daughter, and the whole church treats them that way. They are welcomed and put into active service. Many of them adopt a new lifestyle and find jobs and new friends after they taste the forgiveness and salvation from their Creator. They were put to work at their former trades, using their God-given talents to build the church. And after they had built the church building, some went out and got skilled jobs and even a contractor's license. I can see them now, carpenters and truck drivers, nurse's aides and hair dressers, jazz musicians and teachers. They are like the host that John saw, that no one could number.

The worship there in that church is so powerfully nourishing that all kinds of people come and gladly mix together. They have members who are major corporate execs, who work with addicts and tithe and rejoice like everybody else. When I watch that church, I have a hard time staying up where I belong. It's such a joy to see this church.

I just want to shout when I see or hear about that church and other churches that reclaim and restore those lost ones. Oh, yes, there is a balm in Gilead, a balm in your city, in your land—to make the wounded whole, to heal the sin-sick soul. I pray for you! You have a heavy assignment. But our God will tell you what to do. Just look to Jesus. I know what Jesus did for me. And I count it all joy! Joy! Joy! Hallelujah! So long for now! I will be praying for you! Hallelujah! Hallelujah! Amen.

Question: Among the most controversial issues in contemporary Christian ministry is the question of how far we should go to help people. Prophetically speaking, is the typical Christian, and the organized church in general, sufficiently concerned about the most vulnerable and brutally treated victims in our society?

Should We Stop and Help?

Normal L. Phillips

Pericope: Luke 10:30-37

But a certain Samaritan, as he journeyed, came where he was; and when he saw him, he had compassion on him (Luke 10:33 NRSV).

As Christians we are faced with the troublesome question of where our obligation starts and stops when it comes to helping people in dire need. We all know too well there are times when our deeds of compassion are exploited. We always run the risk of being had. Or do we? And if we do take risks, does that get us off the hook in the Last Judgment?

As we seek an answer, let me invite you to listen to two meaningful and relevant stories. One is from the Bible, indeed from the very mouth of Jesus. We call it a parable. The other is from today; it actually happened to me. Let's start with Jesus' parable of the good Samaritan from Luke 10:30-37.

A certain man has to make a business trip from Jerusalem down to Jericho. He is alone and apparently on foot. At least, we hear no word of him riding a beast. The road, of course, is rugged and crooked. It descends rapidly from Jerusalem, dropping nearly half a mile before it gets to Jericho. The distance as the crow flies is less than fifteen miles, but there are many hairpin turns, each providing a convenient hideout for thieves. In fact, this road is a robbers' paradise.

Most people know this, so many of them travel in groups, and they carry what we call "protection" in the hood. For whatever reason, our business man doesn't seem to know this, so he goes alone, perhaps anticipating a stimulating hike. About halfway down the road, a small gang of robbers pounces on the man, springing at him suddenly from behind a huge rock. They take his purse and strip him of all his clothing. Then, instead of just tying him up and gagging him so he can't cry for help, these brutal rascals beat him half to death, leaving him nearly unconscious, naked and bleeding in the hot sun by the side of the road. It isn't enough to take this helpless fellow's possessions; these vicious hoodlums have to take his health, his dignity, and very nearly, his life.

There he lies, like dead meat, on a roadside.

As gruesome as this ancient piece of reality may seem, humanity today has not progressed beyond it. An innocent schoolboy can be beaten unconscious for a pair of Air Jordan Nike shoes or a starter jacket. Here in Atlanta, three members of the Dooms gang tortured a girl who wanted to get out of the gang. They covered her with bleach, stabbed her, put salt in the wounds, and then set her on fire. The reality described in Jesus' parable is paralleled daily in our world, and most of us have no notion just how awesomely horrible it can be, that is, until it happens to us or to someone in our close circle. I guess my own concern really blossomed only after it happened to me.

I was on my way home from Bible study and had slowed my car down and stopped at a light. Suddenly my car window was broken, and a man slid close behind and put a gun to my head. I had been carjacked. He ordered me to drive to a secluded place, and then with cold, deliberate precision, he raped me and stuffed me in the trunk of my car. The feeling of terror was utterly indescribable, but it didn't rob me of my habit of calling on the Lord for mercy. I was able to keep my wits about me enough to find a button that released the trunk lid. When he eventually stopped the car, I jumped out of the trunk and frantically ran to the cars right behind my car. The rapist drove away. I was not sure whether he saw me escape, but that same night my car was found burned. The rapist had torched the car to destroy the evidence, and maybe to destroy me. But my life was saved!

Well, now let's go back to the Jericho Road and see how our half-dead traveler is faring. He is barely conscious, and his blurred vision has just picked up the image of gorgeous priestly robes, undulating with the movement of the beast on which the priest is riding. He thinks, "Surely this godly man, who is immune to robbers' assaults, will help one who just didn't know how dangerous this road could be. But wait! He is staring hard at me; maybe he will help . . . Oh, no! He has just steered his beast to the other side of the road. He must suspect this is a trick, and maybe he fears he isn't as safe as he had thought in his priestly garb. Or maybe he doesn't want my blood smeared all over his magnificent vestments when he stands before the holy of holies. Or maybe he just doesn't want to be late for his appointment at the church. Sigh! Whatever, he surely isn't slowing down. In fact, he just pulled on the reins and made his animal quicken his pace."

Our traveler lies there a while longer, aching and bleeding, when he sees another churchman, a Levite, a helper to the priests. The traveler thinks, "This one isn't so richly dressed, but he is no beggar. Maybe he will help me. He is gazing at me quite intently. But no! He too has directed his beast to the other side of the road, and he is digging into the poor beast's sides to make him speed up. I guess this Levite is also afraid of being attacked. Or maybe he's not anxious to risk getting blood on his clothes, or being late to a meeting at the great First Church of Jericho. I wonder just how important those meetings really are. And if the very servants of God won't help me, who on earth will?"

The traveler is completely at the mercy of whatever traffic

comes down the road. And so are all who are mistreated, abused, and helpless in a strange place. No one is waiting to care for the wounded—or standing by to protect them in the first place. Our traveler's predicament is timeless and well nigh universal.

Two seminary students of my generation went on a required "plunge." Their school required them to live as homeless people on the streets of a great Eastern city for something like three days with next to no money. Unshaven and bedraggled, as was also required, they sought charitable assistance at a famous church served by a famous humanitarian pastor. They were referred first here, then there, and finally they were denied assistance altogether.

Looking pitiful and worn, and crushed by the attitude at the church, they were wandering down a street just a few blocks from the church when a man stopped his car and offered help. He could see they were sad, and he guessed they were hungry, so he offered to take them to his church, where they could easily be cared for. They asked him which church that was, and his answer really jarred them. When the kindhearted man heard that his church was the church they had just left, he burst into tears. He had thought that a part of his tithe was going to help just such people, and this news about his highly prized church family nearly broke his heart.

The institutional reaction to the needy is all too often mirrored in the way individual laity respond to need. This, too, I know all too well. Resuming my own story, here I was, clothes torn, terrified, running up to drivers' windows, pleading for help. I was passed by car after car in this middle-class community. The drivers had all the earmarks of the typical residents of the area; they were clean and well dressed and dignified. They drove nice cars. A huge percentage of them just had to be good church members and professing Christians. But no one would stop, no, not one. I was seen as a crazy, half-nude human being, someone to avoid at all costs.

This, too, is the measure of a reality of our times. The majority of the folks on our Jericho Roads are as preoccupied as were the folks in Jesus' parable. They have other, supposedly much more important things to do. Lives might be at stake, or innocent people might be enduring unbelievable horrors, but someone else will have to take the time, bear the burden, and run the risk to help, especially when the risk appears to be this great.

Now comes Sam the Samaritan down the Jericho Road. He is part Jew and part original Canaanite, so his skin is dark and his clothing is different. And, of course, he is hated by the Jews, who will have nothing to do with Samaritans. And most of the time, Samaritans return the favor. The two ethnic groups have been hostile to each other ever since Israel's elites were forced into exile in Babylon, and the rest of the folks were allowed to stay amidst the ruins that were left. Jews said Samaritans were, well, just different—and ethnic mongrels. You know how that is. The Samaritan Jews mixed their blood with Canaanite blood, and their faith and worship with that of the Canaanites. Obviously, we can't expect much from this Samaritan fellow.

But look! He's stopping and getting down off his donkey. Would you believe? He's over there bending down and checking that traveler's pulse. And he's covering him with his cloak and dressing his wounds! Wow! Talk about kind and compassionate! Doesn't he know the risks? Isn't he in a hurry too? This black fellow just seems to have kindness in his bones. He's lifting that traveler up and putting him on his donkey. In fact, he's taking him to a motel and paying for his care in advance. He's even promising to pay any balance due when he comes back through. This brother is something else!

Jesus ends the story here and tells his respectable lawyer friend, his deeply religious seeker, to go and do likewise.

The good news for today is that there are still a few good Sams here and there, both individuals and whole compassionate churches. There are still people and entire congregations who know they can't help all the world's crushed and broken, but who don't use that for an excuse to escape from rescuing and helping anyone whatsoever.

A few days ago, Bill and Camille Cosby came to dedicate a multi-million-dollar, state-of-the-art building, an instructional facility they were giving to Spelman College. In his remarks, Bill recalled a compassionate scoutmaster who had bought uniforms for all the boys in his troop when the boys couldn't buy them for themselves. Bill's jokes on other programs make it plain that these scouts weren't little angels, but they had need, and their scoutmaster responded. We are used to seeing him in his role as a comedian, but Bill was dead serious and even tearful when he recalled how he got that uniform he wanted so badly and couldn't buy for himself. That scoutmaster can never know the impact his act had on places like Spelman College.

And yes, I'll move on. You're dying to know what happened to me out there pleading for help on a well-traveled street. Well, thank God, I ran across the street to a car wash. I saw a man running to his car. He drove to me and opened his door, but before I could sit down, another man had flagged down the police, and I got in their squad car. A young woman peeped into the car and asked if she could join me. The police agreed hesitantly, and this woman, Darlene, sat down beside me. I burst into tears, and she comforted me, almost as if I were a baby. She told me she had been raped, but nobody would believe her because they knew she used crack cocaine. There are many excuses for avoiding people on the road to Jericho.

When the police were ready to take me to the scene of the crime, Darlene and the two men said good-bye. They hugged me, and I thanked them most sincerely. Later that same night, I found out that the car wash was a drop off place for drugs, and I realized that my "good Samaritans" were probably crack cocaine addicts. But they stopped what they were doing and treated me with godly compassion and love such as I had never received from a stranger in all my life.

Now I am healed of the trauma that gripped me from that ghastly, unspeakably horrible experience. The scars will always be there, of course, but I have gone back to my labors with the joy of knowing that God loves me so much that I was somehow marvelously spared. I know also that all the Christian people and congregations are not like the priest and the Levite, or the big city, church folks who looked at me in my moment of greatest need and passed by on the other side.

God has a remnant of compassionate people who just can't help being what they are. These are often the people whom we least expect to give compassion, people like the Samaritan. I think I've always been in the remnant, but I am dead sure that I will do my best to grow and become even more compassionate as the years roll on. With the help of the Holy Spirit, I'd like to be like the folks in another story Jesus told.

In Matthew 25, we read that the Lord was commending some people for feeding and clothing and visiting him, and they didn't even know when they did it. They said, "When did we ever see you hungry and feed you? When did we ever see you thirsty and give you something to drink? And just when did we see you naked and clothe you? Or homeless, and took you in? And we sure didn't visit you in no jail!" But the Lord insisted, saying, "Well, inasmuch as you did it to one of the least and last and most needy and oppressed of these, you did it to me. Come, ye blessed of my Father, inherit the kingdom prepared for you from the foundation of the world."

Question: Does a Christian woman keep the peace by quietly submitting, or does she take the initiative and make things happen?

Spiritual Empowerment: A Closer Look

Classy Preston

Pericope: John 20:11-18

Mary Magdalene came and told the disciples that she had seen the Lord, and that he had spoken these things unto her (John 20:18).

I love to hear stories about women, any women, who have overcome. As I grow older I am particularly intrigued by the way our mothers, grandmothers, and sisters have persevered. African American women have had the same obstacles as other women, with the additional burden of race and class. Our ancestors were treated as personal property without regard for our human rights, emotions, or thoughts. But somehow these women were able to survive. I have to wonder how they managed, but not for long, because their songs and stories tell how their unflagging spirits were sustained by faith. These ancestors knew even then, in the midst of unspeakable horrors, that God was with them and that God would somehow work it all out for good.

While growing up in Alabama, I witnessed the hand of God in the life of my grandmother. She lived in a small town, and we would visit during the summer. Her home was a safe haven where a person could experience God's presence, peace, and serenity. Quite often, we would experience powerful thunderstorms. When the storms came, we had to come inside and settle down. As the thunder roared around us and the lightning lit up the sky, we children would cower under the covers. But my grandmother would be pacing up and down the floor, back and forth, back and forth, mumbling words we couldn't make out.

We would watch my grandmother as she walked around the house, seemingly mumbling to herself. I believe now that what we heard wasn't mumbling but rumbling, like the rumbling that rolls after the lightning. This rumbling was a sign that something powerful was going on. My grandmother was tapping into her power source, Jesus, through the guidance of the Holy Spirit. The mumbling was just the working out of the day's problems, turning over to God the many afflictions of her soul. After the mumbling and rumbling was over, she was ready to go on another day.

I have seen the working of the Holy Spirit in my own home. My mother exhibited quiet strength and dignity as she attended to the needs of our immediate and extended family. Her relationship with God resembled the familiar pattern my grandmother had established. Now, in my own more mature years, I find myself beginning to understand the unique dialogue God has with women.

In a recent training seminar, one of the key topics was empowerment. The facilitator observed that this concept, which encourages responsibility and accountability, was a new one in the corporate world. While listening to this, my mind drifted back to the summers of my youth in my grandmother's living room. I also reflected on women throughout history. I began to see that while empowerment might be a new concept for corporate America, it is not new to women, especially African American women. Throughout history African American women have drawn on their spiritual resources for empowerment.

This principle of empowerment manifests itself in our private spiritual lives and in the way we interact with each other and with God. But spiritual empowerment, because it has such concrete results, has become risky business for women, especially those involved in kingdom service. For instance, the spiritual freedom of women is still often subject to challenge, and sometimes outright rejection, even though women continue to prepare for ministry through formal education and vocational training. And spiritual liberation for women is still frequently postponed by the establishment and culture as a matter of supposed convenience for the brainwashed women. When our churches and communities do not support the work of women, even though their work is clearly worthy kingdom service, tensions are inevitable. If women seek to express their spiritual empowerment under these circumstances, they take a risk and might experience lingering negative effects. Women simply can't assume their spiritual gifts will be accepted and appreciated.

As a consequence, many women are often still looking for an acceptable space, one void of oppression, attacks, and exclusion. Many other women, however, witness to their spiritual empowerment daily through testimony, works, and endurance. They say the benefits of freedom in Jesus are far greater than the burdens of opposition and rejection by humankind.

When we view the biblical history of women, we see evidence of spiritual empowerment. The lives of Joanna, Susanna, and Mary Magdalene, women healed of evil spirits and infirmities, attest to the powerful workings of the Holy Spirit. In John 20:11-18, we find the account of the Lord coming to Mary Magdalene in the garden after his resurrection, and we see how she responded to spiritual empowerment. Here is a woman who loved Jesus dearly. Before Mary Magdalene met Jesus, she was on the fringes of society. We don't know many details about her life, but we can guess that her access to ordinary, basic human experiences such as conversation and acceptance (or agape love) was limited, even nonexistent at times. Demonic forces assaulted her body and mind, leaving her seemingly powerless to overcome them. She was a spectator in the game of life with no invitation to participate—that is, until she met Jesus. When she became his follower, she left behind a world of defeat and anxiety. She became a totally different person.

Come with me. Let us go to watch her as this empowered woman makes her way to anoint Jesus' crucified body. It's early, and there is a crisp breeze as Mary Magdalene makes her way to the tomb. The darkness of the morning reflects Mary's grief and loss. When she discovers the empty tomb, her weeping interrupts the stillness of the morning. As she weeps she remembers how Jesus loved her, and she wonders what she will do without him. After all, Jesus healed her and changed the course of her life. Whatever Mary Magdalene's problems had been, her encounter with Jesus has changed her completely and forever. She is a new woman, experiencing spiritual freedom and liberation. Jesus has freed her, and thus empowered and in control, she feels like she simply has to provide for him the amenities and dignities due the departed. It doesn't matter to her who joins her or what anybody else thinks about her actions.

She has begun to feel so empowered that she is willing to ignore social order and customs. Notice that there are two groups of women. One set returns immediately to the city to purchase the necessary spices, while the second group lingers near the sepulcher in deep sorrow. It is Mary Magdalene, however, who runs to get Simon Peter and the other disciple, whom Jesus loved, once again showing her new state of empowerment.

The Gospels mention various other women who were at the scenes of the crucifixion or the empty tomb. No doubt the group of women at the cross and at the tomb included a number who had already played important roles in Jesus' ministry. Some women traveled as part of his band of followers and supported the movement financially. Others had been singularly blessed in his healing ministry. Jesus praised various women profusely for their faith, and in his company many women felt more acceptance and joy than ever before. So it is little wonder that women stood by and wept for Jesus at the cross, and that now they assist with his burial. They were present during those last days and hours because Jesus had been so loving and caring. And given the import particularly of Mary Magdalene's experiences with Jesus, I am not the least surprised that she was there so early and so empowered to lead.

Unfortunately, we do not know much about most of these various women beyond their attachment to the teachings of Jesus and the fact that some of them seemed always to travel together. It appears, however, that these women might have had the wisdom to know that Jesus was their source of spiritual power and to realize how different their lives would be as a result of their connection to the ministry of Jesus.

The Gospel of Luke mentions Joanna at the empty tomb. As she reflected on the significance of Jesus in her life, perhaps she told the others about how she had always attended to the needs of her husband Chuza, in support of his role as Herod's wardrobe keeper. Maybe she observed that her entire identity had been tied up in being his wife, but through Jesus she had found value in just being herself.

Susanna, a follower of Jesus' from Galilee, might have been at the tomb. And perhaps she expressed the joy she experienced by being included in this intimate circle. She rejoiced in their new identities, aware that they had hardly had any identity of their own before. Even in the midst of the trappings of death, they rejoiced in their friend, Jesus, who had given them new life.

Mary Magdalene might have described how her demonic imprisonment had robbed her of control, but Jesus had restored her to balance and power and peace. At the very least, we see that she was set free by Jesus and was then empowered to take initiative and find out what has happened to her Lord. His remains just must be cared for properly, regardless of the ignominious manner of his death. Out of her possessions and limited resources, she did all she had the power to do. Mary Magdalene must surely have been the leader of this little band of women, for she is the only woman mentioned in each account of the resurrection story.

I see her now as she approaches the tomb. We can sense her mounting apprehension as she notices that the stone has been rolled away. She runs excitedly to tell Peter and John, and they together run back to the tomb. Even though they didn't believe her story, Mary Magdalene isn't deterred, because she knows what Jesus has preached, and she takes the gospel seriously, regardless of how strange it has sounded to the disciples. After Peter and John look into the tomb and then go back home, she stays there and weeps, unwilling to leave until she knows what has happened to her Lord. Her complaint to the angels is straight to the point: "They have taken away my Lord, and I know not where they have laid him" (John 20:13).

While Mary talks with the angels, a man she takes to be the gardener approaches her and asks, "Woman, why are you crying? Who is it you are looking for?" Perhaps she asserts, as tactfully as she can, that the gardener had no right to dispose of Jesus' body; the tomb was borrowed, but offered in good faith. "So, sir," she concludes, "if you have carried him away, just tell me where you have put him, and somehow I will go get him and care for him properly." Her tear-stained face belies a driving determination, a spiritual spunk that will not back off for a gardener or any other man. She doesn't know how she will care for Jesus' remains, but she and her sisters will surely do something. Just don't let Jesus' bones lie another minute in some disgraceful heap somewhere, uncared for and improperly mourned.

Now Jesus, whom Mary mistakes for the gardener, decides this exchange has gone far enough. He calls her by name. His voice is like no other voice, and he says her name in a way that no one else could has ever said it. Startled and surprised beyond her fondest imagination, she realizes who he is. She turns toward him and cries out in ecstatic Aramaic, "Rabboni! Master!! Teacher!!!" Mary Magdalene is so happy to see Jesus that she tries to hug him. No Jewish woman should ever do such a thing in public, but Mary Magdalene is a freed and empowered woman, and she forgets for a moment. Who wouldn't?

Jesus says, "Don't hold me now, because I have not yet ascended to the Father, but go to my brothers and say to them, I am ascending to my Father and your Father, to my God and your

God." Still stunned, and yet full of the empowerment bestowed by Jesus, she obeys Jesus' command. Mary Magdalene, the woman once possessed—Mary of Magdala, the nobody Jesus made into somebody—Mary, who just finished fussing with the gardener, starts for the disciples with the news that is to become the core of the gospel for all time and eternity: "I have seen the Lord! He is indeed risen." She can hardly wait. Words form in our imaginations, like: "And let me tell you about that glorious experience when I saw him and talked with him in the garden." But it isn't just the experience in Joseph of Arimathea's garden. It is her entire encounter with Christ uncorked, let loose, never again to be held in.

You see, getting to know Jesus has changed Mary Magdalene's life, and she has become a new woman. It does not matter how she looks on the outside, because Jesus has transformed her within. Mary Magdalene has connected with Jesus spiritually, through eyes of faith in his healing grace. Jesus has taken her from a state of maniacal bondage to one of spiritual empowerment. As she runs to tell the disciples the Good News, she remembers how this man called Jesus has cast out the many demons that have inhabited her life. Jesus has cast out the demon of fear and replaced it with courage. Jesus has cast out the demon of oppression and replaced it with freedom of thought and action. Jesus has cast out the demon of self-hatred, and Mary Magdalene's self-esteem is restored. Jesus has cast out the demon of lust and hate and replaced it with agape love. Jesus has cast out the demon of insecurity and replaced it with a permanent place in the kingdom of God.

The harder Mary Magdalene runs, the more the tears flow, because she realizes that Jesus has been the key to her physical, emotional, and spiritual freedom! She has learned that Jesus is worth whatever risk it takes to gain spiritual power. There is no turning back for Mary. She cannot slip into a state of denial, forgetting who she has become in Jesus, her Savior. The news bursts forth when she finds the disciples. "Jesus is alive! I talked with him in the garden! Yes, I'm sure! And he told me to tell you brothers and sisters that he is going to ascend to his father and our father, to his God and our God."

Two thousand years later, Mary's message is still fresh. We remember how she was moved to rejoice in her freedom. She challenges us today to act on the power God gives each of us, male and female. Spiritual power is a precious privilege that should not be squandered.

The unused spiritual potential of women in our time is a tragic waste in a world desperately in need of the same empowerment that blessed Mary Magdalene. But many women throughout history have risen beyond their fondest hopes by means of spiritual empowerment. One day Wilma Rudolph had to step out, literally, on God's power. Crippled with polio, Wilma was determined to walk again, and through faith and empowerment she overcame. She set the world's record for the 200-meter racing event and exhibited the spirit of a spiritual champion.

The late Barbara Jordan is another example of an empowered woman. She was told that she was not smart enough to be a lawyer. But Barbara stepped out on faith in God and became the first African American to be elected a congress representative from Texas. She also taught at the University of Texas law school. She was a tower of wisdom and strength to the political systems of her time. At her recent funeral, there was not a single leader, including President Clinton, who did not remark—whatever the words used to describe it—about the spiritual empowerment she represented.

Mary Magdalene in the midst of a male-dominated inner circle of disciples was to them what Barbara Jordan was to Lyndon Johnson and his political party.

The world needs sensitive and spiritually empowered women today. It might be that without them, our civilization will falter and die. But with the wisdom and courage with which Jesus empowers the once-suppressed female half of the world's population, our brightest days may yet be just ahead.

Question: Are there people so lost that the church of Jesus
Christ simply should not even try to reach them?

To Seek and to Save

Tina T. Saxon

Pericope: Luke 8:26-39

**For the Son of man is come to seek and to save that which was
lost (Luke 19:10).**

Our communities are coming up with more and more
support groups modeling the parent Alcoholics
Anonymous (AA). Narcotics Anonymous (NA),
prevalent now in some communities, came into being out of the
needs of people who use narcotics. Gamblers Anonymous,
Overeaters Anonymous, Emotions Anonymous, Parents Anonymous, and other groups rise up as people feel the need to confront
whatever it is that has power over them.

Many other programs, some of them government funded, try
to come to the aid of people with a variety of problems that our
society, including our religious communities, has failed to ad-
dress. Some churches have attempted to help by lending or renting
space for these programs in their enormous edifices, but both
parties have agreed to keep a respectful distance from each other.

Drug abuse and its companions, crime and violence, have
virtually destroyed the fabric of decent living in the lives of far
too many African American communities. But who wants to risk
the future of their children, their property, and even their lives to

help, to come to the aid of these people who will do anything for their next fix?

Attempting to use my educational background, my life experience, and my love for Jesus Christ, I responded to God's call to do ministry in an area filled with drugs, violence, crime, and a disrespect for all that is sacred. Working out of a church building proved short-lived. The church people could not and would not involve themselves with the people who surrounded them. In their fear, they turned inward, and they were filled with such anger that they literally mirrored the evil around them.

I concluded that the building is not the church; the people are. A few of us left the building and became a "church" in a public housing development. I accepted a counseling position in a government funded program called Project New Life, a drug addiction day treatment program. I was no longer inside a beautiful church building reaching outward. Now I was in the heart of the demonic, crazed environment that has destroyed so many African Americans that we would rather ignore the situation than face the truth of the matter.

One day I was working with a group in my new "church" space, teaching, counseling, praying, reading Scripture, doing anything that I could think of to spiritually empower these drug addicts. A woman interrupted me with such negative force that I felt the need to pray silently. Because I know the background of some drug addicted people—their short- and long-term jail sentences for theft, assault, and battery, child neglect, shooting, prostitution, defacing public property, hurting their own parents—I did not want to take any chances. The list of things they do in their crazed state goes on and on.

As this woman continued to lambaste me, I thought about how helpless I felt over my inability to really help this group of people. There are too many of them. Some Christian, middle-class black folk who live outside of the inner city are not even aware of what is happening there! And I thought about our people who do *not* abuse alcohol and drugs; they still have many needs for love, compassion, respect and opportunity for a better life. Don't they need my gifts, my talents, my education, too? I stood there wondering, Are we called to hang in there and actually try to reach and heal cases as hard as this?

I knew I had to defuse this situation with this one woman, before it caught fire and spread to others. She shrieked that I was trying to persuade her about *my* God, but *her* God was different. She said I could not persuade her to see God as I see God. My response was quiet, deliberate, and slow: "My God is love. Who is your God?" I was surprised to observe how quickly the tension in the room changed. I felt a stillness and a peacefulness. I was glad we only had a few more minutes before the end of the session.

When the group left, I went to my office and prayed for guidance, courage, wisdom, and understanding. God heard my prayer, for I was directed to a story in Luke 8. Let us turn to it and see if there is a word from the Lord on this mind-boggling question facing the churches: Are there people so lost that the church of Jesus Christ simply shouldn't even try to reach them?

We find in this story a most deranged, dangerous, wild, and fierce maniac. He is so inhumanly strong that he can't even be restrained by chains. He lives apart from society, among the tombs, without shaving or bathing. His clothing is a hodgepodge of dirty, tattered discards. He is a terror to behold, yet Jesus does not back away from this demoniac. In fact, the man does not seem to frighten Jesus at all. But Jesus and the man are not unaware of each other. They are in the same space, the same environment, and they begin to interact immediately. It appears that Jesus has seen the demoniac and acted first. Jesus has communicated something to the man that causes a violent response. Luke tells us when the demoniac sees Jesus, he cries out and falls at Jesus' feet, shouting at the top of his voice, "What do you want with me, Jesus, Son of the Most High God? I beg you, don't torture me" (v. 28 NRSV).

The very sound of his voice strikes terror in me. I begin to wonder, what on earth is Jesus doing in this part of town? Did Jesus go looking for this man who is so deranged that he is thrown out of town, excluded from society, living among the dead?

Whatever brought Jesus and this man together, Jesus is not intimidated or shocked by what he sees. Imagine! Jesus doesn't even blink when this crazy man advances on him. Later on we get an explanation: Jesus says that he came to *seek and save* the lost (19:10).

The people around Jesus, however, feel that this demon-possessed man is too much for them. And no doubt those with Jesus think he has no obligation to deal with people that far gone. They probably feel unsafe around the possessed. Perhaps they also wonder about how much this kind of ministry will drain their meager financial resources. These down-and-outers, Jesus' followers might have thought, are uncouth, dirty, smelly, and very inconsiderate. Their crude selfishness alone does not endear them to the rest of polite society. They do not flush toilets and clean up behind themselves. They ruin the carpets and eat up all the food without replacing anything. These people are too far gone to be helped.

Jesus said he came to seek and save the lost. If dangerous, evil-spirited, violent outcasts of society are not lost, then who are the lost? I believe Jesus meant to save the demoniacs among us—the drug addicts. But this might be too much for our churches.

Jesus, however, felt differently. Jesus claimed no exceptions and fearlessly went against tradition to help the lost.

But let's look at our story again. What a reaction Jesus gets for trying to do good! Jesus commands the evil spirits to come out of the man. Jesus talks with them. They strike up a deal. The demons beg Jesus repeatedly not to order them to go into the abyss. "Please, let us go into the herd of pigs feeding on the hillside." Now, this scene can mess with those of us who eat pig feet and various parts of the pig. It can change our dietary habits, perhaps for the better. Anyway, when the demons came out of the man, they went into the pigs, and the herd rushed down the steep bank into the lake and drowned.

We would expect applause for Jesus. He ought at least to receive a smile and few compliments, but not from this town. The whole town wants him gone. So much for threatening somebody's income and vested interests. What happened? We read:

> When they came to Jesus, they found the man from whom the demons had gone out sitting at Jesus' feet, dressed and in his right mind. And they were afraid. Those who had seen it told them how the one who had been possessed by demons had been healed. Then all the people of the surrounding country of the Gerasenes asked Jesus to leave them; for they were seized with great fear. So he got into the boat and returned. (Luke 8:35-37)

The townspeople were afraid of the healing. So too was the man in need of healing. And the demons had opposed the healing. Why not? When you are out of your right mind, you cannot make wise choices for yourself.

As we look at the man in our story, at first glance we cannot even see a human being. We see the gruesome results of evil. But evil did not attack in the abstract. It used concrete tactics against real people. Why did this man live in the tombs, apparently comfortable in his condition? Why did he think that Jesus' concern for his well-being meant torture? Psychologists and others have an answer: There was something rewarding for him about his condition. They call it "secondary gain." Maybe he liked the attention and power he derived from his craziness. Maybe he enjoyed scaring people and having no responsibilities. Maybe this "secondary gain" from his condition was enough to cause him to be afraid of and to oppose any help he could get. Being healed might mean he would lose something. Evil and derangement lived on because of advantages they provided.

Likewise, our drug addicts of today certainly get a lot from being sick. They get attention. Money from federal programs gives them a place to hang out all day long waiting for a "cure." When they relapse, the whole drug-based, underground economy celebrates their disease. Relapse is part of the program. When they return, they are given so much time and attention that we would think there are more advantages to relapsing than staying free of drugs or sober from alcohol. Besides, dope spares having to feel the pain of life. When a person stays clean, he or she might have to work for a meager salary or take care of children, clean the house, and submit to a husband. Prostitution, drugs, and the "good life" are painless in their way. Addiction has its rewards—short-lived and destructive though they might be.

The drug addict cannot accept God as love, as friend, healer, savior, or helper. Although addiction has its rewards, addicts must also find someone to blame for their condition. God is a good candidate. So are those closest and most concerned about the addict's welfare. ("My wife was so unfaithful after all the money I gave her. It hurt me so bad that it caused me to use drugs to get over the pain.") Staying mad at God, church, parents, or spouse spares the addict from being angry at self for not being responsible and accountable. ("So what if I have these five kids. My mother can take care of them. After all she's their grandmother. She's supposed to take care of them.")

Are these people so lost that the church of Jesus Christ should not even try to reach them? Mere people in a church building are unable to save the lost. Without Jesus Christ as their personal Savior, they too are lost. With Jesus, things are possible if we only believe.

Jesus' power was sufficient just as soon as he made it clear that he had identified the demon by name. Jesus asked the man, "What is your name?" "Legion," they replied, because many demons had gone into him. The man knew he was possessed, and the demons knew it was all over if Jesus ever went to work on them. They knew and feared the power of Jesus Christ. Addicts know they are addicts. Drug addiction is demonic. Drug demons fear recognition and the confrontation of spiritual presence in general. Demons are cunning; they seek to scare us into submission to them before we realize how afraid and impotent they are before a spiritual presence.

The demons were disarmed when unmasked and identified by Jesus. Impossible as it seems, the real person did emerge in our text. He emerged in response to unflappable care and understanding from Jesus. Oh, what power our churches could have if we could unmask and identify the drug addict by disarming him with our love.

Celebration: The healed man was so happy, he wanted to stay with Jesus. Luke tells us, "The man from whom the demons had gone begged that he might be with him, but Jesus sent him away, saying, 'Return to your home, and declare how much God has done for you.' So he went away, proclaiming throughout the city how much Jesus had done for him."

The response was similar in our Project New Life class. They all rejoiced as one of their own from an earlier group returned to our spiritual empowerment group. She came in just to say hello to the new group of students and to give them encouragement. She told them, "I want you to know how happy I am. I have Jesus in my life. Reverend Saxon had a hard time with me when I first came. I did not want to hear about no Jesus. But I have him now in my life. He has saved me. I go to church, and I love it. I put that man out of my life that was helping me do drugs. I want you to know it's about spirituality; it ain't about no programs."

I wanted to shout. Jesus is able. The addict may resist, kick and scream, and rail against God's love and power. But underneath is a person who wants to sit dressed and in his right mind, at the feet of Jesus. Thank God for Jesus! Jesus saves even the wretch undone. Jesus can save the most deranged and dangerous, the wildest people we know, just as he did in our story. Thank God that the Son of Man is come to seek and save the lost!

Question: In view of the endless demands of needy people, all of them from circles far removed from "ours," is there a point beyond which we Christians simply have to draw the line, no matter how sincere the faith or urgent the plea of the needy? Also, how much protection from the pressure of the crowd should a popular, charismatic minister desire or accept?

They Called Him Bartimaeus

Maxine Merrick Walker

Pericope: Mark 10:46-52

And Jesus said unto him, Go thy way; thy faith hath made thee whole. And immediately he received his sight, and followed Jesus in the way (Mark 10:52).

When Jesus was on his way to Jerusalem for the last time, on his way out of Jericho he met a blind fellow I know, Bartimaeus. I haven't any idea how long Bartimaeus had been blind, for he was blind when I met him. And, of course, he very definitely could not see Jesus.

Old Bart was not happy about begging. He would greatly have preferred to get a job, but nobody hired blind people. And besides, what kind of work could he have done? He was commonly known around town as Blind Bartimaeus the Beggar, a title he hated with a passion. People tolerated him to a point, but he was as low on the social scale as a person could get. Being a beggar, he couldn't afford decent clothes or the basic necessities of life. He barely survived off the pittances that fell in his cup. He was never allowed at social functions, and even on the temple grounds he was made to feel like a nothing. He craved just ordinary acceptance. After all, he was not blind by choice. Having to depend on others was no picnic for Bartimaeus. Some people were outright cruel to him; their scorn was due mostly to the fact that he was dirty most of the time, and in need of a serious bath and a hair cut. He just had too many obstacles to overcome: sightless and shunned, poor and unproductive. He would have done anything to avoid begging.

He never told me very much about his family. Obviously his father's name was Timaeus. I didn't dare ask, because he had so much pride, but I just guessed his folks were all dead. And there was nobody else in the temple or the palace who took care of such people in those days.

But Bart was a survivor; he didn't give up. He was what you might call a real tiger. He flatly refused to give himself a never ending "pity party." Even though there were many who thought he was a poor excuse for a human being, he stubbornly clung to his personhood, and to the hope that somehow, someday, things would change for the better. So he kept on surviving, he kept on begging, and he kept on waiting and hoping.

Bartimaeus didn't just wait, though. He watched for an opportunity to be treated and healed. He heard about this prophet and healer named Jesus, and he listened for news of a day when Jesus might come down this very road. This particular day Bartimaeus sat by the roadside waiting, for Jesus was rumored to be coming by soon. He chose a good spot at the side of the dusty road, close enough so that he wouldn't have to fight through too much of the crowd when Jesus actually passed by. He had gotten up early that morning and prepared himself for what he knew would be a great struggle, just to get to Jesus. But he was ready!

Bart knew there was a great chance of being trampled by the eager, selfish crowd. He knew for sure that nobody was going to help him get to Jesus. They all would be trying to get help for themselves. He dared not assume that he could find Jesus by listening, for the crowd made too much noise. He knew also that he stood a big chance of getting lost and disoriented. But he had heard of Jesus' compassionate healing of others. That was why the crowds were so great in the first place. He guessed, indeed he deeply believed, that if he could get in earshot, so that Jesus could hear him, Jesus would hear and help. And he knew he did have a very loud voice.

So he would use that foghorn voice that had cried so long for mere pennies, to cry for healing of sight. There was a certain satisfaction, in spite of his handicaps, in using what he had, even if it was only a loud voice. He could seek help on his own. He would get to Jesus direct. In his mind he said something like, "What he's done for others, surely he will do for me." He was determined that he wouldn't give up until he had at least presented his plea. No matter how rough people made it for him, he was not about to give up short of his goal. He just couldn't give up. There was no time for self-pity. His mind was set on a blessing. He was going to do like Jacob, who wrestled with the angel until the angel blessed him. In fact, he couldn't even imagine that he would be denied. The big problem was simply to get into Jesus' presence.

Excitement was beginning to build up among the crowd as they sensed that Jesus of Nazareth was coming up the road. Bartimaeus began to brace himself. It was a crushing throng that pressed around Jesus as he approached where Bartimaeus was sitting. And Bart had that sharpened "other" sense that made him fully aware of the surging host. He waited for just the right moment. It took audacity to think that he could get the attention of Jesus in this crowd. He was an insignificant beggar. But it also took the right moment. He kept saying to himself, "I came for a blessing, and I'm not leaving until I get one."

Suddenly he sensed that Jesus was as close to his spot as he would ever be. He opened up with that foghorn voice, "Jesus, son of David, have mercy on me." He repeated his plea over and over.

The crowd was surprised and shocked. How dare such an outcast defective yell at Jesus, to say nothing of bursting their eardrums and trying to get ahead of them in the healing line! They were quite irritated and annoyed. They resented what they took to be his intrusion, and many of them yelled back at him: "Shut up! Who do you think you are? You're just a raggedy nothing of a beggar. A lot of nerve you have to disturb the Master. Can't you see you're intruding. Go away, he doesn't have time for you."

This wasn't what you could call encouraging. But Bartimaeus paid no attention to this. It was his only chance, his great opportunity, and he cried out that much louder. He wasn't about to let the crowd cheat him out of getting his blessing. He was desperate, and his voice was quite durable. "Thou Son of David, have mercy on me!" The crowd, likewise, was just as determined that Bartimaeus would not interfere with Jesus' ministry to more important people. He was just a beggar, and he was becoming a nuisance. But the more they shouted at Bartimaeus to be quiet, the louder he got, and the more insistent he became. Bartimaeus knew what was at stake. He just kept calling out, "Jesus, son of David, have mercy on me!" It wasn't polite, but it sure was passionate.

Suddenly the crowd's attitude shifted. Over the noise of the crowd, Jesus had heard Bartimaeus cry. In fact, he had heard more than just one cry. Jesus was touched by the urgency in this cry, and he called for the people to let Bartimaeus through the crush of the crowd. Now they were saying, "The Master wants to see you. Come quickly." He could hardly believe his ears.

All of Bartimaeus's hurts, disappointments, and feelings of inferiority had rung out in Bart's cry. But Jesus was also moved by the force of his appeal, his certainty that help was possible from the hands of the Master. Jesus actually stopped! He stood still! He told the crowd to call Bartimaeus. Jesus turned his attention from all those "somebodies" to the one everyone thought was the least of them all, my friend Bartimaeus. They were shocked, but they called Bartimaeus as Jesus commanded them to. Sheepishly they said, "Cheer up. He's calling for you to come over to him."

When they told Bartimaeus that Jesus had called him, he got so excited that he took off running. He was afraid he might stumble on his robe, so he threw it off. No matter that this very robe had kept him warm and shielded him from the weather. No matter that it was his only robe. There was something much more important, and every second counted. Jesus had called him, and guided by his ears, driven by his determination, he covered the short distance in no time at all. Jesus had called him. He had to respond.

Bartimaeus knew that the opportunity he had awaited for so very long was here. The sight he so desperately needed was something he knew only Jesus could give him. It wasn't money or a job or any of these material things. He was seeking a whole new life. So, when Jesus called, Bartimaeus did not hesitate; he jumped up before Jesus had a chance to change his mind. He just ran, excited, heart pounding fast, all the while making his way to Jesus. He wasn't going to let anyone or anything hinder him. He didn't care about the robe. He didn't care about what the people were saying. He was all caught up in this chance of a lifetime.

When Bartimaeus got up to him, Jesus asked, "What would you like for me to do for you?" Just like that, no preliminaries. And old Bart answered right back: "Lord, I want to see, I want my sight! I want to be able to see all the things I've heard so much about." The crowd was flat out amazed when Jesus said, again straight out, "Go your way; your faith has made you whole." And would you believe it? Right now—immediately—Bartimaeus received his sight. Jesus told him to, "Go your way," but Bart wasn't about to leave Jesus this quickly. Instead of following Jesus' direction to get on with his life, he wanted to follow Jesus himself. He must have been thinking something like old Job in the Bible: "'I have heard about you with my ears, but now I see you for myself, with my own eyes.' And I'm not going anywhere just yet."

And it wasn't just the healing. Bartimaeus talked and talked about meeting Jesus just as a human being. "When I saw him, I was surprised. I don't know what I expected—someone taller, perhaps more muscular. But when I saw him, I saw a man not too tall, small in frame, with very curly hair. Jesus didn't look much different than the other men there, except for his eyes. Suddenly seeing for myself, I can't explain his eyes. There was something about them. They were penetrating and riveting. They looked weary from his journey, but there was something else, something that made me tremble all over. It looked like all the hurt and the sufferings of the world could be seen in his eyes. Those penetrating eyes that seemed to look beyond what eyes are supposed to see. It was as if he knew everything there was to know about me. I know this sounds crazy, but it was like his gaze reached the innermost recesses of my heart. Those eyes, I'll never forget those eyes. And through it all, to think he took the time to hear my plea and help me! Wow!"

Bartimaeus was certain that he was going to follow Jesus wherever he went. Nothing else mattered. This average-looking man with gentle voice and dusty clothes, was telling him with his eyes that he cared. He didn't look at Bartimaeus's clothes. He didn't mention his body odor; he didn't ask about Bartimaeus's family. Jesus was moved by Bartimaeus's determination and faith in him, despite his blindness. It was as if Jesus was telling my friend that he was pleased with him. Nobody else had treated him that way. No wonder he wanted to follow Jesus.

I am reminded of when I met Jesus. I too had heard about him with my ears, but when I found him for myself, I too found a friend. He didn't care what I was wearing. That didn't matter. He didn't seem to mind that my family was poor. None of those things mattered. The only thing that mattered was that I, like Bartimaeus, came seeking help from him. I didn't have to explain how I got in the shape he found me in. He was able to look beyond my faults and he heard me cry.

Jesus is calling the church to be a healing refuge, the place where those rejected by society are welcomed and made whole. The church is called to feel the pain and suffering of the past, to hear the desperate cries of its people in this present time, and to prepare the church for the future. The church is called to instill hope and to discover for all kinds and conditions of humanity the promise of the abundant life. The church must emulate Jesus. It must recognize the cry and call out to those who desperately seek Jesus. It must seek to save, heal, nurture, and love the least of us. All the souls who cry out in pain and suffering echo the voice of

Bartimaeus and the church that hears and responds to the cry of the beggar, hears and responds to the voice of Jesus.

When Jesus responded to my cry, I was reminded of an old familiar hymn sung in the little country church I grew up in, the church where everybody mattered. There was a blind man who was brought to church every Sunday. And there was old lady who had to be helped up the old unsteady wooden steps. Everybody was poor in material things but rich in grace. They would sing that hymn as though they didn't have a care in the world:

Amazing grace, how sweet the sound,
That saved a wretch like me!
I once was lost, but now am found;
Was blind, but now I see.
Twas grace that taught my heart to fear,
And grace my fears relieved;
How precious did that grace appear
The hour I first believed.